# William Shakespeare
# The Comedies

## Twayne's English Author Series

Arthur F. Kinney, Editor

*University of Massachusetts, Amherst*

TEAS 489

# *A* PLEASANT

## Conceited Comedie

### CALLED,

## Loues labors loſt.

As it vvas preſented before her Highnes
this laſt Chriſtmas.

Newly corrected and augmented
*By W. Shakeſpere.*

Imprinted at London by *W.W.*
for *Cutbert Burby.*
1598.

TITLE PAGE FROM THE FIRST QUARTO OF *LOVE'S LABOR'S LOST* (1598).
*By permission of the Folger Shakespeare Library*

# William Shakespeare
# The Comedies

Ronald R. Macdonald

*Smith College*

TWAYNE PUBLISHERS
An Imprint of Simon & Schuster Macmillan
NEW YORK

Prentice Hall International
LONDON  MEXICO CITY  NEW DELHI  SINGAPORE  SYDNEY  TORONTO

*William Shakespeare: The Comedies*
Ronald R. Macdonald

Twayne Publishers
An Imprint of Simon & Schuster Macmillan
1633 Broadway
New York, NY 10019

Library of Congress Cataloging-in-Publication Data

Macdonald, Ronald R., 1943–
  William Shakespeare : the comedies / Roland R. Macdonald.
     p.   cm. — (Twayne's English authors series : TEAS 489)
  Includes bibliographical references (p. 143) and index.
  ISBN 0-8057-7010-0 :
  1. Shakespeare, William, 1564–1616—Comedies.   2. Comedy.
I. Title.   II. Series.
PR2981.M285   1992
822.3'3—dc20                                          91-33736
                                                       CIP

The paper used in this publication meets the minimum requirements
of American National Standard for Information Sciences—Permanence
of Paper for Printed Library Materials. ANSI Z3948–1984. ∞™

10   9   8   7   6   5

Printed in the United States of America

*To the happy memory of*
*Louise Russell Macdonald*
*and*
*Adèle Middleton Russell*

# Contents

# Editor's Note

Beginning with the initial Greek sense of comedy as *komodia,* derived from both *komos,* ritual, and *kome,* village, Ronald Macdonald draws on an impressive array of cultural documents—in anthropology, psychology, and sociology as well as in literary theory and criticism—to show how Shakespeare's own comedy draws on its ancestral pedigree. Macdonald argues that through grafts, joins, and juxtapositions, Shakespeare fuses the two symbolic areas of the early Greek comic stage—the *locus* of realistic character and the *platea* of ritualistic archetype—in ways that through shifting liminality suggest a range of meanings fundamental to life itself. "Comic identity is always a matter of some fraction of the social collective, the marriage, the nuclear family, the court or the city," he writes; "The notion of being in Shakespearean comedy is always tied up with the notion of belonging." But much of the stress of his comedies, as the strain of life, comes in an oppositional pull toward the individual, the solitary, the exiled, the alienated. "Shakespeare's complex sense of identity as simultaneously individual and communal" gives his work much of its enduring force and power: "In Shakespearean comedy," despite a fundamental human tendency, "the self alone is simply not a viable proposition." What follows is a rich, fresh study of all Shakespeare's comic plays, with critical commentaries at once accessible and sophisticated, transparent and hugely suggestive. Macdonald shows how the early plays—such as *The Taming of the Shrew* or *Two Gentlemen of Verona*—were important to Shakespeare's growth as a thinker and artist, while for the mature comedies there are new readings that are as useful as they are memorable. Insights here abound; in *A Midsummer Night's Dream,* he writes, "Puck is the imagination's way of domesticating and ordering the random"; *The Merchant of Venice* is a study of the suppression of both monetary and spiritual economies; the characters in the main plot of *Much Ado about Nothing* misread the subplot so that much of the play's "noting" is about its own actions. *As You Like It* is seen as a combat between the dialogue of liberty and free play and the monologue of the tyrant and the satirist, a play of the provisional. *Twelfth Night* is a play where characters come to realize that when they take on postures and disguises they are not only wasting time, time is wasting them. At once ranging in its ideas and tightly focused in a review of Shakespeare's text, this study will illuminate the plays on the first reading—and yield up further insights on later readings, no matter how familiar or unfamiliar the plays may seem to us at present.

Arthur F. Kinney

# Preface

The 10 plays treated in the chapters that follow represent all of Shakespeare's work traditionally called comedy with the exception of the three late, dark comedies: *Troilus and Cressida* (1601–2), *All's Well That Ends Well* (1602–3), and *Measure for Measure* (1604). These have come to be called the "problem" plays, and they will be treated in a subsequent volume in this series. The first 10 plays form a body of work more varied than the single label "comedy" might lead one to suppose, but it is still coherent, thanks in part to the remarkably stable collection of formulas and type characters stemming from the work of the Athenian comic playwright Menander in the last quarter of the fourth century B.C. Shakespeare's comic production is a remarkable stroke of work, and virtually all of it will repay close attention. I have treated seven of the first 10 comedies intensively and in what I would like to think of as some depth. Constraints of length precluded treating all 10 in this manner, and it seemed to me better to offer individual essays of some substance rather than a rapid and purely descriptive survey. The only justification I can offer for the plays selected for extended treatment is that they seem to me the more substantial and are in my impression the ones most frequently taught. Opinions will no doubt differ on these matters.

For this study I have used *The Riverside Shakespeare*, edited by G. Blakemore Evans et al. (Boston: Houghton Mifflin, 1974). I am familiar with this text, I admire it, and I think the supporting material particularly helpful. But it is by no means the only good edition of Shakespeare in general circulation, and the reader using a competently edited modern text should find no difficulty in locating passages cited below. I have omitted the square brackets that mark variant readings, emendations, and editorial interpolations in the Riverside text.

A project like this one inevitably and happily involves the advice, the encouragement, and generally the sympathetic ears of friends and colleagues. William Oram has read most of what follows and made suggestions with his customary lucidity and generosity. His help is always more than welcome and his friendship highly valued. Camille Paglia, who in a sense got me into this project in the first place, is not the sort to persuade someone to jump off the high dive and then quietly make her own departure by way of the ladder. If she thinks something is a good idea, she goes on thinking so and behaving accordingly. My colleague Gillian Kendall has been most patient in letting me go on about this project, and she has generously contributed ideas from her own work on the late romances. Three other colleagues, Craig Davis, Douglas Patey, and Eric Reeves, have consistently enriched my work through conversations of all kinds, whether about Shakespeare or not. Murray Kiteley gave me aid and comfort in various matters philosophical and logical, and, as I now know, I mention him gratefully by using his name. Nothing can really go without saying, but if anything could, it would go without saying that my wife Marian's companionship, patience, sense of humor, and literary intelligence are not things I could very well do without.

The two women named in the dedication have made a special contribution to this book. The first read me Charles and Mary Lamb's *Tales from Shakespeare* at a time when I could read for myself, I suppose, but not very much. This made a deep impression on me, and the memory of the woman responsible for it continues to do so. The second, who just happens to have been the mother of the first, read some piece of Shakespeare most of the days of her long life, and she inspired in me a sort of *imitatio aviae* to go with an already well-entrenched *imitatio matris*. Such nativity!

# Chronology of Comedies

The date of no Shakespearean play is completely firm, but the dates below rest on both external and internal evidence. The given date is that on which the play first took something like its present form, not the date of first publication.

# Introduction

The roots of comedy doubtless extend far back into the prehistory of Greek civilization, many hundreds of years before the rise of the theater as an institution in the fifth century B.C. The Greek word *komodia* may come from *komos,* a revel or carousal, or alternatively from *kome,* a village. If, as some think, *komos* itself derives from *kome,* then the word may have originally referred to a village revel. If Aristotle is right in his assertion that comedy "originated with the authors . . . of the phallic songs,"[1] then we may be sure that such village revels were obscene in character, involving costumed participants wearing enormous artificial phalluses, and that they were probably part of some ancient fertility rite. In one of the few Greek comedies extant, the *Lysistrata* of Aristophanes, male characters actually do wear such phalluses (they are aroused because the women have staged a sexual strike as a means of ending the war with Sparta), and this may well be a reminiscence of the ancient revel that is comedy's ancestor.

Comedy, at least that distinctive version of it that has come to be called Old Comedy, flourished in ancient Athens in the last quarter of the fifth century side by side with tragedy. Though we know perfectly well that more than one man wrote comedy (Eupolis and Cratinus, for instance, of whose work 46 titles and hundreds of fragments survive), only 11 complete plays of the brilliant Aristophanes are extant. They give us a pretty clear idea of what Old Comedy must have been like. Plots were on the whole skimpy, fanciful, and unrealistic. Great prominence was given to the comic chorus, who interrupted the action periodically to chant long odes known as *parabases* that were only loosely connected, if at all, to the business in hand. The *parabasis* of Old Comedy was obscene (nothing against it, after all, and arguably something for), topical, and very funny, and it often made venomous fun of prominent public figures, some of whom were doubtless in the audience. The introduction of Socrates in the *Clouds,* ensconced in his *phrontisterion* or "thinkery," is only the best-known example of such personal lampooning. The Aristophanic *parabasis* is certainly among the greatest achievements of ancient Greek poetry, though it contributes to a comic spectacle very unlike the one to which we are accustomed.[2]

Aristophanes himself outlived the heyday of Old Comedy and survived into the fourth century. The two surviving plays he wrote in the 390s and

380s, the *Ecclesiazusae* (Women in the Assembly) and the *Plutus,* already show signs that Old Comedy was fast turning into something else, now called Middle Comedy. The two Aristophanic examples are much stronger in plot than his earlier work, and the role of the chorus is increasingly curtailed. Not one example of true Middle Comedy survives: literary history for most of the fourth century is sketchy indeed.

Just after the middle of the fourth century there was born at Athens the man named Menander, who in his career of writing comedy for the stage would fix the genre in the form from which virtually every succeeding instance of stage comedy in the Western tradition would stem. Old Comedy died intestate and without heirs. It left no mark on the subsequent development of the genre. But Menander's New Comedy provided the formulas that have been continuously reworked and varied by comic writers for the stage since Menander's death in the early years of the third century B.C. Here we find the plot that has served and still serves so many Western comedies: boy meets girl and falls in love, boy loses girl, boy gets girl in the end.[3] And here we also find the range of stock characters—tricky slaves, heavy fathers, shrewish wives, braggart soldiers, and the like—that has supplied stage comedy with its people ever since.[4] The title of the one Menandrian comedy to survive in its entirety (there are many fragments, several of them substantial enough that the whole play may be easily reconstructed), the *Dyskolos* or *Curmudgeon,* gives some idea of the direction in which the concept of character in New Comedy is headed.

It was from the vast Menandrian corpus of well over 100 plays that the two great practitioners of Latin comedy, Plautus and Terence, largely drew in creating their own comedies.[5] It is in their work that Menandrine comedy has really come down to us, and, of great importance for the case of Shakespeare, their work came to occupy a central place in the humanist curriculum of the sixteenth century. If Shakespeare really did attend the grammar school in Stratford, he may well have read there the *Menaechmi* of Plautus, the play that became the basis of his first comic effort, *The Comedy of Errors.*

When Shakespeare first came to London sometime around 1590, he entered a world already buzzing with literary activity (if that had not been the case, he might not have come at all). Plays were being written not only for the recently founded public theaters (the first was built in 1576), but also for coterie productions in the universities, the schools, the Inns of Court, and similar venues. While there had been drama in England for centuries by Shakespeare's time, theater (if the distinction may be allowed) had only existed for a comparatively short span, and public theater as an independent, admission-charging enterprise, a profit-making business like any other, for a very short span indeed. But enthusiasm ran high, as the number of plays and the building of new theaters attests. Already active by the time Shakespeare arrived were such men as George Peele and Robert Greene, two members of the circle called the University Wits that included the great tragedian Christopher Marlowe, all graduates of Oxford and Cambridge who wrote plays they sold to troupes of actors to be played in the public theaters. Peele is perhaps best known for his comic play *The Old Wives' Tale* (first published in 1595) and Greene for his *Friar Bacon and Friar Bungay* (published 1594), a comic version of the Faust legend probably inspired by Marlowe's tragedy on the same theme.[6] At the same time John Lyly was writing comedy in a more ornate and academic vein with plays like *Alexander and Campaspe* (published 1584).

Such men, whatever their merits, were hardly a pioneering vanguard. Comedy had been developing rapidly in England since the time of the Tudor accession, and the first half of the sixteenth century saw plays like John Heywood's *The Play of the Wether* (published 1533) and Nicholas Udal's *Roister Doister* (published 1566, but probably written 1553) that were still popular at the end of the century. Shakespeare thus had a rich heritage at his disposal, and it included not only existing stage comedies but a native and largely oral tradition of popular clowning, mummery, and folklore. No small part of his peculiar genius is expressed in his ability to fuse disparate strains of comedy in the same play: when the metamorphosed Bottom meets the Queen of Fairies in *A Midsummer Night's Dream,* we have a veritable icon of his eclectic and syncretic abilities that is visual as well as linguistic, a virtual dialogue between courtly and popular forms of entertainment.[7]

The popular traditions of clowning and mummery mentioned above remind us that Shakespeare also had at his disposal a double acting style that he often exploited to great effect. Robert Weimann has made a fascinating argument that Shakespearean drama (and Elizabethan drama in general) draws on both a tradition of mimetic representation (the realistic style to which we are accustomed, with the actors as characters ignoring the presence of an audience) and a nonmimetic representation to which belong asides to the audience or even extended direct address, foolery, jigs, and improvised clowning.[8] Clowning and buffoonery are characteristic of what Weimann calls the *platea,* originally simply "the street," but more generally the site where the play is staged. Mimetic representation, on the other hand, is characteristic of the *locus,* the stage metamorphosed by the imagination of playwright and audience into a fictive locale, where characters (in this style our awareness of the underlying actor will tend to recede) are engaged in interchange one with another but not with the audience. Shakespeare worked with a bare platform for a stage, surrounded on three sides by members of the audience. The arrangement conduced admirably to a fluid relation between the styles of *locus* and *platea,* allowing an opportunity to shatter dramatic illusion at will (it is a vulgar misconception that the playwright always aims at a perfect illusion), as well as to restore it when meaning so dictates. To continue the example of *A Midsummer Night's Dream,* when at the beginning of the third act the "translated" Bottom wearing an ass's head puts his companions to terrified flight, he is left alone on stage to speak a few grumbling words about what he takes to be their joke on him and sings a song to keep up his spirits (III.i.120–33). Here we are very close to the pure clowning of the *platea,* but when the song awakens Titania and she is instantly smitten, there ensues a dialogue that is certainly far closer to a genuinely mimetic encounter. *Locus* and *platea* interpenetrate, and once again we have a fusion of learned and popular traditions.

It is not, of course, the case that no other playwrights wrote such hybrid drama with varying degrees of success, only that Shakespeare was unquestionably the most skillful of them at making such grafts and joins and juxtapositions work for him to produce complex meanings. And he was not (fortunately) above poking fun at earlier and clumsier attempts at such mixtures. The title-page of Thomas Preston's tragedy in the old-fashioned "ranting" style, *Cambises* (ca. 1569), for instance, describes it as "A lamentable tragedy mixed ful of pleasant mirth, conteyning the life of Cambises King of Percia."[9] When Peter Quince in *A Midsummer Night's Dream* calls the artisans' dramatic effort *The most lamentable comedy and most cruel death of Pyramus and Thisby* (I.ii.11–12), which later becomes "A tedious brief scene of young Pyramus / And his love Thisby; very tragical mirth" (V.i.56–57), we are justified in suspecting that Shakespeare is having some fun, if not with Preston's play itself, at least with plays of its kind. Four or five years later in *1 Henry IV* he would have that incomparable improviser Falstaff offer to act the part of King Henry in a play ex tempore: "I must speak in passion, and I will do it in King Cambyses' vein" (II.iv.386–87). If in the event "Cambyses' vein" turns out to sound suspiciously like the ornate prose of John Lyly, so much the better, for the hilarity is only compounded. No one is likely to protest a little inconsistency (especially the intentional kind) in anything this funny.

Falstaff's improvisational skills are shared by nearly every other Shakespearean comic hero or heroine (especially the heroine), by the more knowing fools like Touchstone in *As You Like It* and Feste in *Twelfth Night* and, as one inevitably guesses, by their creator as well. Shakespeare was anything but a classicizing snob (there were plenty around in this period of revived interest in classical literature), and he must have felt genuine admiration for masters of improvised foolery such as Richard Tarlton, who also acted, wrote plays, and was so skilled a swordsman that he became master of the fence in 1587. His skills of the *platea*, in the theater and elsewhere, soon became legendary. Shakespeare must have also admired the man who played clowns and fools for his own company in the later 1590s, Will Kempe, who was famous not only for his mimetic acting skills, but for a series of "merriments" (that is, short passages of improvised repartee) and jigs. He left Shakespeare's company in 1599, possibly to make time for his next escapade, a nine-day dance marathon from London to Norwich, in which he danced a morris along the entire route between the two towns. The project (if that is the name for it) actually took a month (unlimited rest periods were allowed between days), but Kempe actually did dance along nonstop all day for each of the nine days of his progress. It was he who had brought off with such aplomb that perennial theatrical feat in the part of Bottom—a supremely skilled actor successfully imitating a decidedly unskilled one.

Shakespeare seems to have connected improvisational skill with flexibility and adaptibility, the ultimate comic virtues (tragedy, on the other hand, requires of its heroes an uncompromising, unswerving, and ultimately deadly commitment—think of Macbeth or Othello). Survival and growth are for the comic vision matters of strategy, shrewdness, and the capacity not to take the self too seriously, and as a result, the foe of comic festivity and merrymaking is inevitably a rigid, unswerving type who takes himself seriously indeed. "Art any more than a steward?" Sir Toby asks the censorious and agelastic Malvolio in *Twelfth Night* (II.iii.114–16), "Dost thou think because thou art virtuous there shall be no more cakes and ale?" Although Malvolio's strictures have something to be said for them (Toby is rather overdoing the revelry), nevertheless the first question hints at his overbearing ambition (a form of rigidity that can sometimes get itself confused with a wish genuinely to grow and change), while the second suggests his adherence to a formulaic morality he would impose on others. Neither aspect harmonizes well with a world in which people ideally have more than one way of surviving, like plants that have rings of undifferentiated tissue capable of becoming, as the need arises, leaf, stem, or root.

Set over and against such sour killjoys as Malvolio are figures like Viola, the heroine of *Twelfth Night,* and Feste the professional fool. Instead of Johnny One-Note, we have in Viola someone who can "speak . . . in many sorts of music," as she herself puts it (I.ii.58), and in Feste one who can juggle multiple roles and play them all simultaneously to perfection. Northrop

Frye, following the anonymous author of the ancient treatise known as the *Tractatus Coislinianus,* who was himself following the lead of Aristotle, has reminded us that comic action can be described as a contest between the *alazon* or impostor and the *eiron* or self-deprecator, with the latter invariably triumphant in the end.[10] Self-deprecation is simply one form of not taking the self too seriously, and in Shakespearean heroines and fools it is normally expressed as the willingness to abandon a self, a single, invariable, often calcified, and always illusory entity to a series of brilliantly acted roles. The heroine disguises herself as a boy, and in *As You Like It* this yields the rather vertiginous spectacle of a boy actor (all female roles were taken by boys in Shakespeare's time) playing a girl, who proceeds within the fiction to disguise herself as a boy, who then proceeds to impersonate a girl, who has the same name as her(?) own(?).

There is always complexity in the disguised Shakespearean heroine, even when it is not a matter of the layered roles of Rosalind's performance, because the heroine, who is always an *eiron* in her own person, invariably impersonates an *alazon* in disguise. In discussing her scheme for fleeing the court with Celia, Rosalind alludes to the archetypal *alazon,* the miles gloriosus or braggart soldier:

> Were it not better,
> Because that I am more than common tall,
> That I did suit me all points like a man?
> A gallant curtle-axe upon my thigh,
> A boar-spear in my hand, and—in my heart
> Lie there what hidden woman's fear there will—
> We'll have a swashing and a martial outside,
> As many other mannish cowards have
> That do outface it with their semblances.
>
> (I.iii.114–22)

And Portia in *The Merchant of Venice,* in speaking with Nerissa of her planned disguise, promises, once she is dressed like a man, to "speak of frays / Like a fine bragging youth, and tell quaint lies" (III.iv.68–69). If neither pushes her scheme to the extreme she merrily anticipates, the fact remains that each is in the odd position of impersonating an *alazon* or impostor, a kind of imposture of imposture with which Shakespeare plays some pretty complex games.

One of the effects of the heroine's imposture in Shakespeare's comedy is to render as role what is a matter of serious behavior among other self-deluded

characters in the play, usually male. This effect might be called a comic catharsis: when the self-deluded see what they take to be their own natural
behavior parodically rendered, they may further see that what they have understood as a matter of necessity is really a matter of choice and come off it.
Once again, the comic vision aims at banishing rigidity and establishing the
conditions for flexibility and freedom, however qualified the concept of freedom must be.

But it is time to move on to the plays themselves. Let it be noted in conclusion that the foregoing remarks are necessarily sketchy and have no
pretensions to exhausting the topic of Shakespearean comedy or foreclosing
discussion, qualification, or even outright objection. There are certainly ex-
ceptions to virtually every generalization offered here, and for every reformed
lover one can find an unreconstructed curmudgeon or killjoy left over at
play's end, a kind of surd element that refuses to be factored in. Shakespeare
certainly suffered no delusion that comic solutions are also magical ones, and
if there will always be those who are, as Jaques says at the end of *As You Like
It,* "for other than for dancing measures" (V.iv.193), there is not much that
anyone, the playwright included, can do about it. And at both beginning
and end of the span of years in which Shakespeare produced comedies for the
stage he wrote plays that do not really fit the patterns discussed here. The
early *Comedy of Errors* is, as we shall see, not really a play about romance at
all, and the later *The Merry Wives of Windsor* is about married life rather
than romance, if the distinction can be made without undue cynicism. Comparisons, as Dogberry, the determined constable on duty in *Much Ado about
Nothing* remarks, are odorous. One can only hope that the comparisons offered above (and the ones below, for that matter) will at least not turn out to
be fishy.

## Chapter One

# The Comedy of Errors: After So Long Grief, Such Nativity

Although some have argued that *The Comedy of Errors* is the very first play Shakespeare wrote, it is more likely his fourth or fifth, coming well into or after the first historical tetralogy.[1] There is a reference extant to a performance of the play at Gray's Inn, one of the Inns of Court, during the Christmas festivities in 1594,[2] and while this need not have been its premiere, it seems likely to have been. One reason that the notion of *The Comedy of Errors* as Shakespeare's first play is so attractive is that this comedy anticipates in brevity and dramatic craft his last play, *The Tempest*. In both he strictly observed, as nowhere else, the classical unities of time and place. It is tempting to think of Shakespeare as dramatically self-conscious from the very start, bracketing his canon with academic examples of classical dramatic practice (just to show that he could perfectly well do it when he so chose), and meanwhile pursuing in the body of his work his own idiosyncratic way. This just-so story is almost irresistible, and yet resist it we must. It is not entirely consonant with the historical record, and we must doubt in any case that Shakespeare thought in terms of creating a canon. Though the notion of a Shakespearean canon is convenient for scholars, it remains doubtful that Shakespeare himself, involved as he was with every concrete aspect of the theater from writing to production to acting, had it as a working hypothesis.

Certainly, *The Comedy of Errors* is one of a group of early comedies and possibly the first comedy, if not the first play, that Shakespeare wrote. In the earlier half of the 1590s he produced not only *The Comedy of Errors*, but *The Taming of the Shrew*, *The Two Gentlemen of Verona*, and *Love's Labor's Lost*. This early development of the comic genre is generally thought to have culminated with the brilliant *A Midsummer Night's Dream*, a play that recalls in many aspects the earlier work but also anticipates the mature achievement of the great romantic comedies, *As You Like It* and *Twelfth Night*. If *The Comedy of Errors* is a journeyman's effort, it is nonetheless an altogether interesting one, and it has continued to be viable in performance, amusing and charming to readers, and, as far as the critical tradition is concerned, an object of continuing exploration.

One thing that marks *The Comedy of Errors* as early work is its uncharacteristically close adherence to an identifiable source, the *Menaechmi* of
Plautus, the Roman comic playwright who flourished in the latter half of
the third century B.C., and whose work, along with that of his younger contemporary Terence, formed a staple of the academic curriculum in
sixteenth-century England. Plautus (who was himself doubtless working
with an older play, now lost) provided Shakespeare with the basic situation
of separated identical twins, one brother in search of his long-lost counterpart, and the confusions that result when both twins, unbeknownst to one
another, find themselves in the same city. Shakespeare, of course, made
some changes (his play is in no sense a translation of the *Menaechmi*), some
minor, some of greater consequence. Most obvious, he redoubled the original Plautine doubling by giving his twins, the Antipholuses, twin servants
as well, the Dromios, thus vastly multiplying the opportunities for confusion.[3] And we may note a change of place. Though Shakespeare's twins, like
Plautus's, are born of Syracusan parents, the "lost" twin resides in Ephesus,
not the Epidamnum of the original. The switch may have been in part motivated by his wish to include the debate between Adriana and Luciana concerning the proper behavior of wives (II.i), an exchange that draws heavily
on the Apostle Paul's advice in Ephesians 5:21–33; or again, by the metaphor of witchcraft and conjuring, practices attributed to the Ephesians in
Acts 19:13–20.

But even this apparently inconsequential change of place reveals some
important differences in outlook and ethos. The very facts that the status of
wives is debated in Shakespeare's play and that Adriana is at last brought by
the Abbess to insight about herself in the final scene sets *The Comedy of Errors* apart from its classical source. The corresponding wife in the *Menaechmi*
is a stereotypical shrew: she has no inner life, evokes no sympathy, and is left
to be auctioned off, along with the Epidamnian Menaechmus's other goods
and chattels, when he decides to return to Syracuse with his newly found
brother. The *Menaechmi* is undoubtedly funny, but it is also by our standards rather hard and cynical, for it presents a world in which everything,
including human beings, has its price. Indeed, we may suspect that coinage
is Plautus's central metaphor and that the notion of interchangeable twins is
something akin to two coins of the same denomination. Either is equally ne-
gotiable in the same transaction.

Although Shakespeare's twins, particularly the wanderer from Syracuse,
are not without a certain opportunistic venality, their world, if not doctrin-
ally Christian, has an atmosphere very much within a Christian ethos. The
marriage of the Ephesian Antipholus and Adriana, for instance, though vis-

ibly strained, is nonetheless posited as a basic value, and it takes an extraordinary circumstance, nothing less than being inexplicably locked out of his own house, to drive Antipholus of Ephesus to take his midday meal at the house of a courtesan. His Plautine counterpart, on the other hand, regularly and habitually patronizes a neighboring courtesan, nor does his wife seem much to mind, as long as he refrains from stealing her things to give to his mistress and continues to pay the bills. Sixteen hundred years of Christianity, and particularly 60 years of Shakespeare's Protestant form of it, with its emphasis on the sanctity and centrality of marriage, have clearly had a softening effect on Plautus's cheerfully cynical vision.

That *The Comedy of Errors* contains a good many farcical elements no one will doubt, for Shakespeare has scattered generously those staples of farce—sight gags, pratfalls, and beatings—throughout his play. But that it is therefore to be classified as a farce pure and simple is a more problematic conclusion.[4] Robert B. Heilman has reminded us that true farce is "an automatic result of banana-peel incidents. Things happen to people more often than people make things happen. In sum, farce elects to depict the human being at a stage where he has not yet taken on the burdens of mind, feeling, conscience, and will."[5] In the world of Plautus's *Menaechmi* we do seem to begin with the premise that people are things, commodities, really, that circulate in the Epidamnian economy alongside goods and services. If the play ends with a partial release from this status, summed up, perhaps, in the manumission of the Syracusan Menaechmus's slave Messenio, it is still that same former slave (and the institution of slavery is the essential expression of people as commodities) who as a free man conducts the auction of the Epidamnian twin's household effects, including his wife. However fanciful that last detail may be, it still has considerable metaphorical force in defining the nature of the Plautine world.

With Shakespeare's play, it seems more accurate to say that he begins not with the premise of people as things, but with a situation, and a highly unlikely one at that, capable of reducing people to things, and then, in a last-minute surprise for which even the audience is wholly unprepared, reveals that situation as capable of restoring to them something like the impression of full and individual humanity. It must be admitted that the very notion of doubling in twinship mightily assists the sense of commodified humanity, for the presence of identical human beings inevitably suggests that people are created with some kind of cosmic cookie-cutter or are mass-produced by being struck from the same die.[6] And yet for Shakespeare (and he returned to this in his other twin comedy, *Twelfth Night,* as well as elsewhere) the idea of achieved identity, at least in comedy, always involves some idea of doubling or plurality, because comic identity is always a matter of some fraction of the social collective, the marriage, the nuclear family, the court, or the city. Perhaps the text from Ephesians that struck him most, even more than Saint Paul's advice to wives, occurs in the fourth chapter where Saint Paul affirms that "we are members one of another" (Ephesians 4:25).[7] The notion of being in Shakespearean comedy is always tied up with the notion of belonging.

Perhaps Shakespeare's complex sense of identity as simultaneously individual and communal can be made to seem somewhat less paradoxical by reflecting on our own use of the term "identity," for we undoubtedly use it to denote both an individual and a group phenomenon. On the one hand, we use the term to point to those characteristics that mark a person as unique, the kind of thing included on an ID card: thumbprint, photograph, date and place of birth, and the like. On the other hand, we speak, without sensing a contradiction, of an individual "identifying" with a group, that is, of deriving a sense of self from the collective that shares his race or religion or ethnic background, for instance. Modern usage implies a dialectical relation between individual and group and suggests that they are interdependent concepts rather than mutually exclusive categories.

In Shakespearean comedy the self alone is simply not a viable proposition: the isolated individual cut off from the ties of communality may not only be vulnerable to death, he may actively desire it. Such is the case with Egeon in *The Comedy of Errors*, as he enters believing himself utterly bereft of family and friends and commanding the duke to make short work of him: "Proceed, Solinus, to procure my fall, / And by the doom of death end woes and all" (I.i.1–2). And a curious detail in his long expository speech, as he describes the storm that has begun his woes, clinches the point:

> For what obscured light the heavens did grant
> Did but convey unto our fearful minds
> A doubtful warrant of immediate death,
> *Which though myself would gladly have embrac'd,*
> Yet the incessant weepings of my wife,
> Weeping before for what she saw must come,
> And piteous plainings of the pretty babes,
> That mourn'd for fashion, ignorant what to fear,
> *Forc'd* me to seek delays for them and me.
> (I.i.66–74; emphasis added)

It is only Egeon's sense of connection to his family that prevents him from embracing "immediate death" and forces him to find the means of salvation.

Thus, if Plautus uses doubling largely as a means of farcically reducing his characters, Shakespeare uses the doubling device to more complex effect. For if doubling is inevitably reductive in *The Comedy of Errors* (especially when the doubling is itself doubled), it is also part of a larger meditation on the problem of identity, an extreme instance of the play of likeness and difference through which a workable sense of self is finally attained. The Shakespearean process of finding a viable identity entails an anterior experience of losing a less-developed, less-satisfactory one, rather as a snake sheds the skin it is beginning to outgrow. A relatively primitive organization enters a liminal period, where it encounters not only chaos and confusion, but also a saving fluidity, wherein old rigidities are dissolved and new possibilities can emerge.[8] In the later romantic comedies this liminal period is normally indicated by disguise, literal or figurative. The heroine dresses up as a boy and self-consciously explores the masculine potential of her nature. The hero typically embraces some form of delusive behavior, plays the roles it dictates (without, however, being aware of them as roles), and, with rather less sophistication than the heroine, tries out extreme postures in order to appreciate finally the rewards of a more temperate and balanced one.

There are, of course, no disguises of this kind, either literal or figurative, in the early *Comedy of Errors,* only the identical twins. But they are so often taken for one another that by stretching a point each might be said to be disguised as the other. There is yet this crucial difference: the masquerades of the later comedies are uniformly the result of conscious schemes and unconscious desires on the part of the characters themselves. But in *The Comedy of Errors* confusions and mistakings are divorced from the wills of the protagonists, for those confusions are generated by the improbable situation alone. Nowhere else in the comedies is agency quite so purely impersonal.[9] And yet the aim (which in this case must be attributed to a benevolent fortune or chance, and finally to the playwright)[10] remains the same. An old self, encrusted with habit and a fairly rigid set of assumptions about the world and its workings, is lost to the ultimate benefit of a new self, more complex, better integrated, and more flexible. We shall see in the concluding section of this chapter that *The Comedy of Errors* is a special case, in that the new self attained is actually an even older self that has been superseded. But the process of attaining it remains basically the same, and the Syracusan Antipholus foresees it without being aware that he is doing so, when he deploys for the first time in the play the kind

of figurative language that constitutes one of Shakespeare's most important additions to his Plautine original:

> I to the world am like a drop of water,
> That in the ocean seeks another drop,
> Who, falling there to find his fellow forth
> (Unseen, inquisitive), confounds himself.
> So I, to find a mother and a brother,
> In quest of them (unhappy), ah, lose myself.
>
> (I.ii.35–40)

If this dissolving of the boundaries that mark the limits of the individual is
here imaged as a kind of death, it nevertheless anticipates the reunion with a
larger whole, the return to one's familial native element, which is the individual's ultimate perfection in this play.

The body of the play, of course, necessarily consists not of reunions and
reconciliations, but of divisive mistakings, innocent errors that constantly
generate anger and the threat or fact of comic violence. No sooner has the
Syracusan Antipholus, for instance, delivered his affecting complaint than
the Ephesian Dromio enters to bid the man he thinks is his master home
to dinner. The incident initiates the series of mistakings that will become
the play's stock-in-trade, assuring a beating for the Syracusan Dromio in
his apparent failure to perform his original errand, and anticipating the
cross-purposes that will generate four further beatings for the two servants, not one of them merited. The wonder is that no one tumbles to the
truth in the course of "this sympathized one day's error" (V.i.398). The
heroine of Shakespeare's later twin comedy, Viola, guesses the truth at the
first hint of a mistaken identity (*Twelfth Night,* III.iv.375–76), and while
it is true that her brother is not only of the opposite sex, but has a different
name, the speed with which the potential problem is disposed of suggests
that by this time Shakespeare has found subtler and more varied ways of
generating a comic plot.

But he has not found ways any funnier. Though *The Comedy of Errors* can
seem a one-joke sort of affair, the humor is in fact frequently complex and
genuinely sophisticated. Take the first exchange at cross-purposes, where
Ephesian Dromio implores Syracusan Antipholus to return to a wife and
home he has in fact never heard of:

> The capon burns, the pig falls from the spit;
> The clock hath strucken twelve upon the bell:

> My mistress made it one upon my cheek:
> She is so hot, because the meat is cold:
> The meat is cold, because you come not home:
> You come not home, because you have no stomach:
> You have no stomach, having broke your fast:
> But we that know what 'tis to fast and pray,
> Are penitent for your default to-day.
>
> (I.ii.44–52)

No one would claim that these lines are among the finest examples of Shakespearean blank verse, but the lockstep regularities and repetitions may be part of the point. Dromio sketches a world in which events proceed in orderly and predictable chains of cause and effect, and his repeated "because"s hammer this idea home. What he cannot know, of course, is that he has just entered a situation in which the laws of logic and probability have been suspended, where a cause in one series, for instance, can have an unlooked-for effect in a parallel but apparently unrelated series, as if two trains running at full tilt on adjacent tracks were somehow to swap a few cars in passing.[11] We have an example of such diverted and invasive causality every time one servant is sent on an errand but encounters his master's twin before he returns to his true master. Even at the very outset Ephesian Dromio's orderly causal scenario looks not so much like a neutral description of the way things indisputably work, as it does like an attempt to impose order on a world increasingly resistant to such ordering.

*The Comedy of Errors* anticipates in some ways the weird causality of Laurence Sterne's Shandean world, where a man's passion for constructing miniature fortifications can cause, through an unlikely chain of events, his nephew's accidental circumcision by means of a falling window sash.[12] But although displaced and invasive causality is a large part of the kind of humor Shakespeare includes in *The Comedy of Errors*, it is by no means the whole story. With this same first exchange at cross-purposes we are introduced to a characteristically linguistic dimension of Shakespearean comedy in which language itself, quite apart from those who use it, seems to take up a role in the confusions. No reader will overlook the fact that both Dromios are inveterate punsters. This penchant we might put down entirely to Shakespeare's youthful wish to display a precocious linguistic virtuosity and then deplore for producing tedium more often than admiration. Without disputing the latter (tolerances, after all, differ), we may still have some reservations about the former. The Dromios' wordplay typically involves homophones or near homophones, words that sound alike (and are commonly so spelled), but which have different meanings and are often entirely unrelated. Thus, the noun *post* meaning "haste" and the noun *post* meaning "a stake of wood set in the ground as a marker or support" present the Ephesian Dromio with the opportunity to jump from one meaning to the other: "I from my mistress come to you in post: / If I return, I shall be post indeed, / For she will score your fault upon my pate" (I.ii.63–65).

The joke here, slender enough on the face of it, is nevertheless more complex than it seems, for the phenomenon of homophony is something like the linguistic equivalent of identical twinship in biology. It is popularly supposed that a word, like a man, retains a stable identity wherever it travels. Homophones call this supposition in question, for they force us to see that a word derives its meaning as much from its environment or context as it does from its inherent lexical substance. The trick of the homophonic pun really depends on the punster's conscious and willful switching of contexts; *The Comedy of Errors* works this trick over and over again, in prose as well as in verse:

> Sconce call you it? So you would leave
> battering, I had rather have it a head.
> And you use these blows long, I must get
> a sconce for my head, and insconce it too,
> or else I shall seek my wit in my shoulders.
> (II.ii.35–39)

If the Dromios' verbal agility seems at times somewhat smug, we would do well to remember that the principle of context they have mastered in language is the equivalent of the principle of context that masters them in the action of the play. Every time they adroitly take a verbal identical twin and place it in a new context that changes its meaning, we are reminded that a transpersonal agency is continually doing precisely the same sort of thing with them. The language of the play seems teasingly to trace the solution to the muddle that no one, however improbably, can solve on his own.

What we encounter in the punning language of *The Comedy of Errors* is a dim foreshadowing of a linguistic meditation that Shakespeare would proceed to complicate and enrich in his more mature comedies, and particularly in his other twin comedy, *Twelfth Night*. It is a meditation that can be roughly adumbrated in a question: do we speak in language, or does language speak in us? The answer is unstable, never cut-and-dried, and in *Twelfth Night*, as we shall see, the answers forthcoming are always fertile and frequently poignant. But everywhere in Shakespeare the man who thinks that he controls language absolutely is in for a surprise. And the man who takes the next step and thinks that because he controls language, he therefore controls the world, lets himself in for some version of Hotspur's retort to Owen Glendower, when the latter boasts that he "can call spirits from the vasty deep": "Why, so can I, or so can any man, / But will they come when you do call for them?" (*1 Henry IV*, III.i.52–54). It is considerable food for thought that the man we class quite rightly as one of the very greatest masters of language should return repeatedly to the problems that the will to mastery poses, both in language and in life itself.

In one respect *The Comedy of Errors* is something of an anomaly. When we think of the broad sweep of Shakespearean comedy, we quite naturally think of the process of wooing and winning that leads finally to marriage. Indeed, eight of the 13 plays traditionally classified as comedies take these matters as their focus; one, *The Merry Wives of Windsor* (1600–1601), treats life in marriage; and the three "problem plays," *Troilus and Cressida* (1601–2), *All's Well That Ends Well* (1602–3), and *Measure for Measure* (1604), at least show an intense interest in the increasingly troubled relations between the sexes. It is true that *The Comedy of Errors* explores the problem of married life through the marriage of the Ephesian Antipholus and Adriana, and includes the wooing of Luciana by the Syracusan Antipholus that we are encouraged to think will end in marriage. But this plot strand, it must be admitted, is given pretty short shrift, and Shakespeare keeps the matter barely alive at the end, when Syracusan Antipholus says to Luciana, "What I told you then / I hope I shall have leisure to make good, / If this be not a dream I see and hear" (V.i.375–77). This is not much to hang a romantic plot on.

Clearly, Shakespeare is interested in something else besides romantic love in *The Comedy of Errors,* and in a brief and trenchant essay W. Thomas MacCary has made a brilliant suggestion about what that something else might be.[13] Building on Northrop Frye's argument that romantic comedy always presents some version of the Freudian oedipal struggle, with a son and father, for instance, competing for the affections of the same girl,[14] MacCary argues that the *The Comedy of Errors* addresses the desires and problems of the individual in the pre-oedipal stage of development. Accordingly, the central character is not in quest of an erotic object, but of a mirroring double, the ego ideal established in the early relation with the nurturing mother and the individual's first means of achieving a sense of independent selfhood.[15] We encounter again in slightly different guise the Shakespearean paradox of identity, where individualized selfhood depends on doubleness, and we are reminded that it has been the Syracusan Antipholus's sense of incompleteness that has sent him in search of his other half and set the play in motion.

Thus the conclusion of *The Comedy of Errors* is not union but reunion, not the founding of a new family, but the recovery of an original one, and in this the play resembles the late romances more than the mature romantic comedies:

> Thirty-three years have I but gone in travail
> Of you, my sons, and till this present hour
> My heavy burthen ne'er delivered.
> The Duke, my husband, and my children both,
> And you the calendars of their nativity,
> Go to a gossips' feast, and go with me—
> After so long grief, such nativity!
>
> (V.i.401–7)

This remark of the Abbess, now revealed as Aemilia, mother of the Antipholuses and wife to Egeon, is in some ways strange. Not only does she make the figurative claim to be giving birth to her twin sons once again, but she caps the figure by calling the impending reunion banquet a "gossips' feast," that is, a celebratory meal taken after a baptism ("gossip" has its archaic sense of "godparent"). A 33-year gestation period—even a figurative one—would be long indeed. But the remark perhaps rests on a wish simply to abolish the 33 years of wandering and begin the family de novo, this time on a path that will avoid disaster, shipwreck, and separation. In figuratively reenacting the very first separation—that of the twins from her own body in the act of birth—Aemilia seems to preclude the possibility of further separation in the tortuous byways of the world.

It is just this dialectic of separation and union or reunion that the play recapitulates at every step. It is implicit, for instance, in the affecting words Adriana addresses to the Syracusan Antipholus in the belief that he is her erring husband:

> How comes it now, my husband, O, how comes it,
> That thou art then estranged from thyself?
> Thyself I call it, being strange to me,
> That, undividable incorporate,
> Am better than thy dear self's better part.
> Ah, do not tear away thyself from me;
> For know, my love, as easy mayst thou fall

> A drop of water in the breaking gulf,
> And take unmingled thence that drop again,
> Without addition or diminishing,
> As take from me thyself and not me too.
>
> (II.ii.119–29)

"Farewell, dear mother," the mock-mad (or possibly quite genuinely mad) Hamlet says to his stepfather; and, when Claudius gently corrects him, Hamlet insists, "My mother: father and mother is man and wife, man and wife is one flesh—so, my mother" (IV.iii.49–52). Both Hamlet and Adriana are concurring in their different ways with Saint Paul in his Epistle to the Ephesians: we are members one of another. And it is really no accident that Adriana's imagery here mirrors, with a different emphasis, that of Syracusan Antipholus in his earlier soliloquy (I.ii.35–40). For where his speech expresses a fear of an obliterating union with an undifferentiated element, Adriana's speech asserts the impossibility of separation from that same element. And yet what both fear is a loss of identity, the one in union, the other in separation. As always in *The Comedy of Errors,* true selfhood is the result only of the dialectical relation between part and whole.

We can even understand the framing action of the play (a characteristic Shakespearean graft, incidentally) involving the hapless Egeon under sentence of death as participating in the dialectic of separation and fusion. In one sense this introductory scene is no more than a rather undramatic means of exposition, reminding us that the price of adhering to the classical unity of time is the often inconvenient requirement for expository passages.[16] In another sense Egeon's tragic story is an effective counterpoint to the body of the play, with the very real violence threatening his person, for instance, played off against the caricatured beatings that the Dromios receive at the hands of their masters. Egeon moves in a situation where the impersonal agency manipulating men's lives is politics, a situation, in short, made by men through law, though not necessarily entirely under their control. We have seen that the agency manipulating the situation in the body of the play is something like time or fortune or whatever powers there are that govern coincidence and play jokes on mere mortals. But in yet another sense Egeon's situation is parallel to, not in contrast with, the one in the body of the play, for the draconian legislation mandating death for Syracusans found in Ephesus reduces all Syracusans to a common denominator, deprives them of specific identity and gives them in its place a generic one. From the point of view of Ephesian law all Syracusans are alike, any one is the identical twin of any other. Here, as in the body of the play, Shakespeare works the device of reducing human beings to identical counters but with rather grimmer effect. Egeon becomes the faceless victim of a law in no way motivated by any transgression on his part, and he is deprived of his personal history, even as he recounts it in such specific detail, only to be refitted with one unrelated to him, the brief and sketchy history of the quarrels between the cities of Syracuse and Ephesus.

In Egeon's situation the Pauline dictum that we are members one of another takes on a somber cast, for one innocent Syracusan can easily die for the transgressions of another, the "rancorous outrage" of the Syracusan duke in extorting money from "well-dealing" Ephesian merchants (I.i.5–10). But this is precisely analogous to the kind of substitutions we encounter in the comic sequence, for each of the twins repeatedly and unwittingly walks into a situation where he in effect acquires his counterpart's personal history and has what surely must qualify as the uncanny sense of an unknown Other living his life for him. Freud's notion of the uncanny, developed in his essay of 1919 on the topic, is roughly that the uncanny is the experience of something strange and yet familiar, the unbidden return of repressed knowledge.[17] The idea is surely pertinent here, particularly because a part of Freud's essay deals with the uncanny effects of doubles or alter egos. Following an argument of his colleague Otto Rank, Freud says, "For the 'double' was originally an insurance against the destruction of the ego, an 'energetic denial of the power of death,' as Rank says; and probably the 'immortal' soul was the first 'double' of the body. . . . Such ideas, however, have sprung from the soil of unbounded self-love, from the primary narcissism which dominates the mind of the child and of primitive man. But when this stage has been surmounted, the 'double' reverses its aspect. From having been an assurance of immortality, it becomes the uncanny harbinger of death."[18]

This passage is of considerable interest to the student of *The Comedy of Errors* because it throws light on the regressive aspect of the play, on the fact, for instance, that the twins figuratively return to the hour of their birth (as suggested by the Abbess's odd assertion, discussed above) and, indeed, literally return to their origins, in that they are reunited with their parents. Freud goes on to conclude, "When all is said and done, the quality of uncanniness can only come from the fact of the 'double' being a creation dating back to a very early mental stage, long since surmounted—a stage, incidentally, at which it wore a more friendly aspect."[19] And though he is silent about the details of the process by which "the 'double' reverses its aspect," we may refer it to a very simple fact of human psychology: the more energetically something is denied, the larger looms the threat of its presence;

one can protest too much, as Shakespeare well knew, and thus betray the presence in oneself of the very thing protested.

What the twins achieve with their reunion in the final act is not so much the completion of an erotic quest (that will be Shakespeare's chief comic preoccupation in the later comedies), but the long-lost security of childhood, a time when the self was relatively safe from annihilation, because it was plural, not single, and presented the forces of annihilation with a confusing multiple target. If Shakespeare had given *The Comedy of Errors* a subtitle, it might well have been "Safety in Numbers."[20] In the liminal period of confusions and mistakings the twins endure, the lost and unseen double wears the aspect of a threat to the self, and the Syracusan Antipholus is driven to the extremity of explaining the disruptive effects of the mysterious Other as the result of conjuring and witchcraft. Adriana, meanwhile, chalks what she takes to be her husband's odd behavior up to madness. And the twins well and truly change places, for the Syracusan Antipholus acquires all the benefits of settled life in a larger community, as unknowing citizens press upon him home-cooked meals, gold chains, and the like, while the hapless Ephesian Antipholus suffers a version of the fate owing to his brother (as a Syracusan citizen in Ephesus {I.ii.1–7}) in being bound hand and foot and haled off to the ineffectual ministrations of Dr. Pinch.

When the twins are finally brought face to face, there is considerable relief for those on stage (less so for those watching off stage, because we have known all along the way the thing works), for all threats are revealed as illusory, a kind of trick done with mirrors, including the one that has almost cost Egeon his life. Although the duke at the outset has elaborately denied the possibility of remitting Egeon's penalty (I.i.141–49), he nevertheless refuses the Ephesian twin's offer to pay the necessary ransom and magnanimously frees his prisoner from all forfeits: "It shall not need, thy father hath his life" (V.i.391). The gesture is hardly consonant with the logic of his earlier argument, but it perhaps attests to the regained sense of security that even nontwins can derive from the spectacle of an apparently doubled self. No other Shakespearean comedy is quite so intolerant of loose ends and odd men out (the dreadfully punished Dr. Pinch hardly counts), and the seamless whole that the end of *The Comedy of Errors* presents is a kind of achievement, undoubtedly minor, but still welcome, that Shakespeare would never care to repeat.

# Chapter Two

# The Taming of the Shrew, The Two Gentlemen of Verona, and Love's Labor's Lost

Shakespeare's first effort in writing comedy was followed rather closely by three plays that established—with some hesitation—the direction that virtually all his later comic writing would follow. In *The Taming of the Shrew* (1593–94), *The Two Gentleman of Verona* (1594), and *Love's Labor's Lost* (1594–95) mature erotic and romantic relationships culminating in marriage occupy the focus in a way that makes the treatment accorded this area of experience in *The Comedy of Errors* seem perfunctory indeed. This trio of comedies prepares the way for the brilliant *A Midsummer Night's Dream*, written on the threshold of Shakespeare's ripest comic period.

It is not, to be sure, the case that Shakespeare simply and abruptly abandoned certain central concerns of *The Comedy of Errors* in moving on to later plays. A preoccupation with identity and character, for instance, continues throughout his writing of comedy. But after his first comic play these matters tend to be treated under the aspect of viable erotic relations, which are themselves viewed as the goal of human development and maturation. No longer do comic actions round toward the recovery of a previous state of affairs; instead, they push ahead to a future that, for all that it grows out of a past, we can imagine as discontinuous from it.

But neither is it the case that Shakespeare discovered the paradigm that we have come to think of as most characteristic of his comedies either at a stroke or in the course of some sure and unflinching progression. The three plays to be considered in this chapter, and particularly the first two, reveal a kind of tentativeness and uncertainty in the solutions they embrace, a tendency to explore in directions that would never be taken again in the roughly 10 years of Shakespeare's intensive writing of comedy for the stage. From the point of view of the mature comedies, there are some cul-de-sacs here; once having entered them there was little the playwright could do after encountering the dead end but back out and begin afresh. An important task of what follows will be to suggest some of the things he may have picked up on the way in and out.

*The Taming of the Shrew* is a most pertinent case in point. The story of the main plot, though it can cause a modern audience a good deal of uneasiness, would perhaps have surprised no one who first saw it in the early 1590s. One of Shakespeare's probable sources, an extant play called *The Taming of a Shrew,* is but one version of a common story concerning a willful woman brought to heel; the male fears that underlie such stories find expression even in folkways—the village procession, for example, aimed at ridiculing a shrewish wife (or the weak husband considered her victim) known as a skimmington. Such is the view from the ambient culture looking into the Shakespearean corpus, but if we shift our venue to the inside, *The Taming of the Shrew* begins to look more like an anomaly, something Shakespeare tried early on and then abandoned for good. For the central romantic relationship as it develops between Petruchio and Kate really reverses the emphases of what we must consider the typical relationship in Shakespeare's comedies, where the woman is ordinarily the preceptor (though she does her teaching in male disguise), the man the aberrant or foolish creature who must by some means be brought into line. "I found him under a tree, like a dropp'd acorn," Celia says of the moonstruck Orlando in *As You Like It* (III.ii.234–35), making clear the assumed superiority of females to males, at least in the probationary period of the typical romantic comedy.[1]

Instead of calling in question certain distinctions we normally take for granted, including the distinctions we habitually make between the sexes, Shakespeare was apparently content in *The Taming of the Shrew* merely to internalize the dominant patriarchal ideology of his world in order to confirm it in Petruchio's victory over his fractious wife. This ideology proclaims among other things the "natural" superiority of husband to wife, a hierarchy typically bolstered by analogies with other hierarchies more or less taken for granted and announced as the natural way of things: monarch over subject, aristocrat over commoner, human being over animal—this last, of course, enabling the title of Shakespeare's play.[2]

It is not altogether surprising that this situation, so unpalatable to the modern sensibility, has produced in recent years various kinds of palliative interpretation. One line of argument concedes the coercive, even cruel, elements of Petruchio's treatment of Kate, the draconian methods of his "taming-school" (IV.ii.54), but then points out that the kind of farce Shakespeare was writing typically involves reducing people to the status of

things and manipulating them as such. Since farce always involves a distancing and stylizing of violence, since it encourages a certain anaesthetization of
normal feeling on the part of its audience, we are liberated to laugh at a
spectacle that under different circumstances might disturb or even appall
us.[3] There is much in Shakespeare's text to suggest the validity of this approach, including the fact that some of the protagonists' most outrageous
moments, like Kate's act of breaking the lute over Hortensio's head
(II.i.148–59) or Petruchio's outlandish behavior at his wedding (III.ii.157–
79), are narrated by secondary characters rather than dramatized directly.
Indeed, Grumio's account of the rough-and-tumble misadventures on the
road to Petruchio's country house is rendered, ostensibly to protest Curtis's
interruptions, in conditional sentences, which has the effect of further distancing what is already at a considerable remove from unmediated action:

> But hadst thou not cross'd me, thou shouldst
> have heard how her horse fell, and she under
> her horse; thou shouldst have heard in how miry
> a place, how she was bemoil'd, how he left her
> with the horse upon her, how he beat me because
> her horse stumbled, how she waded through the
> dirt to pluck him off me.
>
> (IV.i.72–78)

Such stylized distancing is at least indirectly related to another line of palliative argument, one that makes somewhat larger claims for the sophistication of dramatic technique in *The Taming of the Shrew*. In this case we are
asked to believe that what Petruchio wants from Kate is not unquestioning
submission and obedience but "play and mutuality,"[4] that Petruchio's aim is
to get Kate to realize that shrewishness is not in one's nature, not some putative ingrained characteristic, but a role adopted according to a choice now
forgotten as such and become "second nature." On this view the change
Petruchio effects in Kate is not much different from the change Rosalind of
*As You Like It* will later effect in Orlando or the one Viola in *Twelfth Night*
will effect in both Orsino and Olivia. In all cases it is the preceptor's problem to try to get his or her subject to take a broader and more flexible view
of the self, to come to the happy awareness that we have more choice about
who we are and what we do than we had supposed, and that one's current
mode of address to the world is hardly the only or inevitable one.

Again, as with the argument from the nature of farce, there is much in
the text that can be taken to support such a stance. Repeatedly, whether

self-consciously or naively, various characters treat Kate's ill-humor and outrageous behavior as if they were a matter of pretense, a put-on for whatever reason. Thus, in response to Kate's evidently unpalatable suggestion that Bianca favors the elderly Gremio among her suitors, the sister replies, "Is it for him you do envy me so? / Nay then you jest, and now I well perceive / You have but jested with me all this while" (II.i.18–20). This may be the last resort of desperation (Kate has bound her sister's hands in an attempt to wring information from her), but it surely prefigures Petruchio's far more knowing way of slyly treating Kate's temper as if it were merely the face she shows the world and not at all an expression of her essential self. When Petruchio blandly announces that the wedding day is Sunday, and Kate snaps, "I'll see thee hang'd on Sunday first" (II.i.299), Bianca's suitors and her father are understandably skeptical about Petruchio's success in wooing. But he is unshaken in his deadpan determination to deny the obvious facts of the matter:

> Be patient, gentlemen, I choose her for myself.
> If she and I be pleas'd, what's that to you?
> 'Tis bargain'd 'twixt us twain, being alone,
> That she shall still be curst in company.
>
> (II.i.302–5)

The key phrase here, perhaps, is "I choose her for myself," for Petruchio means not only that he has chosen Kate as his wife but that he has chosen a version of her, a possible Kate, so to speak, more nearly conformable to heart's desire.

Hamlet, prince of Denmark, possibly the most theatrically preoccupied character in all of Shakespeare, advises his frail mother to "Assume a virtue, if you have it not":

> That monster custom, who all sense doth eat,
> Of habits devil, is angel yet in this,
> That to the use of actions fair and good
> He likewise gives a frock or livery
> That aptly is put on.
>
> (III.iv.161–65)

The gist of Hamlet's advice, however arrogant it sounds in coming from a son to his mother, is perfectly valid: what begins as the pretense of virtuous behavior, its mere acting out, can become with time internalized and automatic, indistinguishable from native virtue indeed. Similarly, we may understand Petruchio's strategy as involving the thrusting of a role upon Kate that she will gradually learn to play to perfection, a process that is clearly prefigured in the "Induction" to *The Taming of the Shrew,* when the Lord arranges to have the role of aristocratic gentleman thrust upon Christopher Sly, who in turn begins to believe (although his belief is quite partial and clearly unstable) that unaccustomed luxury is his true lot in life, his memories of his life as a tinker the delusions of madness merely.[5]

Side by side with the strategy of treating Kate as if her behavior were already mild and harmonious Petruchio also does an exemplary impersonation of an outrageous nonconformist, providing Kate with a hyperbolic parody of her own refractory ways. His cobbled-together costume (III.ii.43–63), his bizarre behavior at the wedding ceremony (III.ii.157–82), and certainly his impatient cantankerousness later on at his house in the country (IV.i, IV.iii) all seem directed at mirroring Kate's own excesses and persuading her to abandon them, to adopt a mode of behavior governed by "modesty," a key term in this play in that it refers both to a social virtue and to an artistic one, the kind of disciplined control the Lord of the "Induction" has in mind when he warns the players about a failure of their "modesties" (Ind.i.94). But both of Petruchio's strategies are at bottom thoroughly theatrical, and they form the centerpiece of a play that is preoccupied with the changes, the substitutions, the crossings and dissolutions of otherwise well-established boundaries that become possible in theatricalized situations.[6] Indeed, so eager was Shakespeare, apparently, to imbue *The Taming of the Shrew* with the plasticity of the theatrical that he included instances of dubious necessity, at least as far as the manifold plots and schemes of the play are concerned. We may wonder, for instance, why the servant Tranio must assume the identity of his master Lucentio, and further why, having taken on his master's role, he must woo Bianca in concert with his master, who is disguised as Cambio. "If thou ask me why," says Lucentio, "Sufficeth my reasons are both good and weighty" (I.i.247–48). We may suspect that his reasons are Shakespeare's and have to do with generating further instances of personal substitution and interchange.

Thus we may choose to see stubbornly rooted positions in *The Taming of the Shrew* happily dissolved in playfulness and theatricality, the world shifting giddily, forming and reforming, as various characters conjure it in imaginative language. There is a delightful exuberance in Tranio "get[ting] a sire" (II.i.411), that is, finding an older man to impersonate Vincentio to Tranio's own impersonation of Lucentio. In his punning on *get* as "procure" and as "beget" Tranio stirs into life the youth's comic fantasy of simply reinventing an older generation to meet the needs of the younger. Such play is clearly related to Petruchio's strategy of treating Kate as if she were already an ideal woman, and Petruchio himself is, of course, the play's past master of improvisation, one who invents and reinvents the world as the situation requires, whose every move reminds us of the techniques of the theater, whether he "thinks with oaths to face the matter out" (II.i.289), or feeds Kate "with the very name of meat" (IV.iii.32)—the only way, after all, characters in a play are ever fed.

But even after noting all the abundant examples of exuberant, self-conscious theatricality on the part of both characters and playwright we shall still be forced to admit that Kate's conversion from shrewishness rests as much on threats and coercion as it does on discovering the joy of playful mutuality. Even a view of the play as generous and sympathetic as that put forth by Marianne L. Novy cannot quite eliminate all taint of violence in Petruchio's bearing toward Kate, and when Novy remarks of the celebrated IV.v that Petruchio "claims the moon is shining, not the sun, and refuses to continue the trip unless [Kate] agrees,"[7] we can only object that Petruchio does something more than refuse to continue the trip. Indeed, he threatens a return to the "taming-school" with its physical deprivations of food and sleep. We cannot speak of a progression from farce to a higher form of comedy here, simply because the farcical threat of violence continues as a way of guaranteeing the pretense of something more refined. And the language that Kate is here bullied into speaking is hardly "determined by her relationship with Petruchio,"[8] except insofar as he is threatener, she threatened. We cannot have play and reciprocity on the one hand and coercion on the other. Coerced play is no play at all but at best the appearance of play.

Critical discussions about *The Taming of the Shrew* will doubtless continue to culminate in interpretations of the fifth scene of the fourth act, as well as of Kate's final speech concerning the duty of wives. In each case there will be debate about the tone of Kate's language in particular, how we are to "take" it, what we suppose the speaker's relation to her words to be. Perhaps no argument about these matters can ever be knockdown or final, but it seems certain that the concluding exhortation concerning the duty of wives can never entirely escape the shadow of coercion and be truly read as a virtuoso performance, part of an intimate and fluid game that Petruchio has succeeded in teaching Kate to play.[9] In the final analysis *The Taming of the Shrew* seems not so much to achieve playful mutuality as to gesture toward it.

A concern with love and friendship and the way that relationships between members of the same sex bear on or compete with relationships between members of the opposite sex remains constant throughout Shakespeare's comedies and is central even to the intense and competitive human drama played out in the Sonnets. "Two loves I have of comfort and despair," the poet says toward the end of the sequence in the 144th sonnet, and he goes on to unfold his suspicion that his "better angel," "a man right fair," has been seduced by a "worser spirit," "a woman color'd ill," in fact the passionate "dark lady" whose presence is so troubling to the poet in the latter half of the sequence. The perfidy sketched in this scabrous little poem is an extreme instance of the kind of tensions everywhere found in Shakespeare's work when the demands of friendship collide with the demands of romantic involvement and there is competition for a finite amount of attention and regard.

The collision tends to compound the problem of mutuality that Shakespeare began to address (perhaps unsuccessfully) in *The Taming of the Shrew,* and in *The Two Gentleman of Verona* the problem seems to overwhelm him at the conclusion. The many inconsistencies and uncertainties of this play (hesitantly dated 1594) suggest early and insufficiently revised work,[10] but the fifth act in particular, with its unlikely band of outlaws (were it not for the anachronism, we would surely fix their provenance in comic opera), its lightning conversions, and generally implausible harmonies is perhaps unrivaled in the canon for sheer awkwardness. But of all the difficulties, surely Valentine's awarding of Silvia to Proteus after the latter's cursory apology for his monstrously perfidious behavior is the most notorious piece of utter fatuity this or any other Shakespeare play has to offer, a desperate attempt to reconcile the conflict between friendship and romantic love that has been rightly characterized as a futile and magical gesture.[11]

The fact is, as W. Thomas MacCary has remarked with something of the effect of understatement, "the play as a whole . . . values friendship between men over the love of men for women that leads to marriage."[12] We sense in this early piece a pronounced skittishness about mature sexual relations that will continue throughout Shakespeare's comic canon, one difference between earlier and later being that in *The Two Gentlemen of Verona* Shakespeare seems to have felt obligated to resolve the conflict between same-sex and different-sex relationships, where in later plays like *The Merchant of Venice* or *Twelfth Night* he remains content with a poignant dramatization of the problems. And where in the later plays he is increasingly explicit about the things young men find threatening in mature erotic relationships, as when, for instance, the Rosalind of *As You Like It* in disguise as the youth Ganymede quite frankly raises the specter of marital infidelity and betrayal, the younger Shakespeare writing *The Two Gentlemen of Verona* contrives or simply allows the play to remain quite silent on the perils of the transition from youthful friendship to mature romance. The reluctance that is given a sufficient rationale in the later plays is left to inference in this early one, and the result is a resolution that seems at best sheepishly arbitrary.

That we do indeed infer reluctance on the part of the two gentlemen of Shakespeare's play comes in no small measure from what one sympathetic analyst has called its "brittle and cool charm."[13] And that particular kind of charm must rest ultimately on a particular kind of style and language in which *The Two Gentlemen of Verona* abounds. Perhaps nowhere else in Shakespeare's comedies are the feelings of romantic love expressed in such a displaced and hypothetical way, and nowhere else are such expressions so easily diverted into wordplay or so casually set aside for the pleasures of bandinage. It is as if the turmoil of passion could be managed and contained by finding apt phrases for it, thus belying Julia's mild retort to her maid's sensible advice: "Thou wouldst as soon go kindle fire with snow / As seek to quench the fire of love with words" (II.vii.19–20). And one result of this curious state of affairs is that attention is diverted from the signified, the feelings presumably attendant on relationships, to the signifier, the language in which those feelings are made known. Surely the mannered elegance that often results is a large part of what constitutes this play's "brittle charm."

At its least interesting this shift of attention results in a dry and programmatic quality, as when Proteus, in a speech that reports feeling but fails to embody it, cooly charts the changes in libidinal investments effected by his first sight of Silvia:[14]

> Methinks my zeal to Valentine is cold,
> And that I love him not as I was wont:
> O, but I love his lady too too much,
> And that's the reason I love him so little.
> How shall I dote on her with more advice,
> That thus without advice begin to love her?
> 'Tis but her picture I have yet beheld,
> And that hath dazzled my reason's light.
>                                        (II.iv.203–10)

What Proteus apparently means by having as yet beheld only Silvia's "picture" is that he has not yet experienced the fullness of her perfection, both outer and inner. But we will scarcely forget that he later begs Silvia for her picture in fact:

> Vouchsafe me yet your picture for my love,
> The picture that is hanging in your chamber;
> To that I'll speak, to that I'll sigh and weep;
> For since the substance of your perfect self
> Is else devoted, I am but a shadow;
> And to your shadow will I make true love.
>
> (IV.ii.120–25)

We are thus led to suspect what Julia, who is present here in disguise, makes explicit in a canny aside: "If 'twere a substance, you would sure deceive it, / And make it but a shadow, as I am" (126–27). Proteus, we conclude, prefers shadow to substance, the imagination of romance to romance itself, endless confabulation about love to love indeed.

This deferring of the substantial is hardly peculiar to Proteus, for we mark it in every phase of a dramatic action that often seems designed to effect separations rather than unions. The plethora of letters and other written communications that is peculiar to this play seems symptomatic of the retreat from signified to signifier. For example, the letter Proteus has written to Julia, for which she feigns contempt in the play's second scene, bids fair to displace the very protagonists who are its writer and recipient:

> Lo, here in one line is his name twice writ,
> "Poor forlorn Proteus, passionate Proteus:
> To the sweet Julia"—that I'll tear away—
> And yet I will not, sith so prettily
> He couples it to his complaining names.
> Thus will I fold them one upon another;
> Now kiss, embrace, contend, do what you will.
>
> (I.ii.120–26)

Further, the letter Valentine has written at Silvia's request to a "nameless friend" (II.i.105) turns out to be the lady's rather coy device for declaring her love to Valentine, thus ensuring that Valentine has written only to himself, a fitting figure for the predominantly narcissistic orientation of desire in this comedy. Language, as the clown Launce's comic "mistakings" suggest, seems more an instrument of isolation and misunderstanding than of union and harmony.

Here again we can observe Shakespeare continuing a meditation we saw him beginning with *The Comedy of Errors,* the reflexive consideration of his recalcitrant medium, of the ways in which language eludes complete subjugation to its users. It is not only that certain characters retreat from the substantial into language, for they are captured by language as well. In a process to some extent inherent in the comic genre, with its remarkably persistent array of stock types, and one that Shakespeare would exploit to far greater effect in *A Midsummer Night's Dream,* characters tend to become subordinate to the conventional roles, postures, and expressions furnished by the romantic and comic traditions.[15] Julia's pretense of indifference to Proteus and his letter in I.ii, the conventional response of a respectable and maidenly young woman to romantic overtures, is a clear instance of the problem of language in this play. Like Viola's male disguise in the later *Twelfth Night,* language has the tendency to "become the form" of the speaker's intent (*Twelfth Night,* I.ii.54–55), to substitute its own logic and direction for those of the person who supposedly controls it.[16] Language, like disguise, like conventional posture, is a servant become master, an agent become principal. With Julia the stance that convention makes available to her, cool indifference, is in fact a falsification of her own feelings, and she is thus divided between the means of expression and what she would truly express, the two being ill-sorted and unfitted to one another.

Julia's dilemma is but an extreme version of the way the means of expression in general tend to distort or displace intention, as in the next scene (I.iii) when her love letter to Proteus is drawn into a chain of events that ends up in separation rather than union, as Proteus is shipped off to join Valentine at the Milanese court. And if Julia is recognized by many students of *The Two Gentlemen of Verona* as by far the most vital and complex character in the play, that may be in large measure because she is the only one aware of the gap between intention and event. While other characters shift from one state to another, one total commitment to another, without apparent depth or memory, Julia experiences something like the anguish that accompanies the consciousness of inconsistency and betrayal. She is no less a creature of the signifier than the other characters: the difference is that she is an unwilling and protesting creature—at least until the notorious finale, when her complexity is abruptly sacrificed to the generically mandated happy ending, and she is implausibly reduced to uncomplaining silence.

It is not altogether surprising that Shakespeare should have meditated from the very start on the distorting effects of all forms of mediation—language, of course, preeminent among them. As a playwright who was also a working actor, he was in a peculiarly good position to observe the warpings and diversions at the various stages of bringing a play before the public, from the initial conception, through writing, casting, and rehearsing, to the final production and the inevitable variations in performance from day to day. Surely it cannot have escaped him that the pristine script that he delivered to his company to embody and present never quite survived this process intact, always underwent some degree of modification or distortion as the sovereign will of the author necessarily ceded control to a plurality of wills, each with its own ideas about how a line, a speech, a part, and the play as a whole should look.[17] Theater is not the only literary medium in which the author's originating will is deflected and refracted by the wills of others (no author, for instance, can entirely control a reader's response), but it is perhaps the only one in which this dispersal is a stage in the process of representation itself, anterior to the consumption of the artifact by the public. Proteus's experience in *The Two Gentlemen of Verona* prominently includes a search for a reliable agent, as he finds Speed, then Launce something less than ideally obedient in performing the tasks he imposes and at last ironically settles on the disguised Julia as a reliable go-between in his wooing of Silvia (IV.iv.62–73). Proteus's frustration may well reflect his creator's, as he was faced with the problem of shepherding his work unchanged through the process of theatrical embodiment. But we may suspect that the creator, unlike his creation, was aware from the start of the impossibility of the task.

An interest in, not to say a veritable preoccupation with, the linguistic medium marks *Love's Labor's Lost* even more than *The Two Gentlemen of Verona*. The later play, tentatively dated 1594–95 and probably revised for performance at court in 1597,[18] is an exuberantly garrulous affair, containing specimens of virtually every fashionable literary and rhetorical mode of the 1590s. The reader approaching this effusive production for the first time may be pardoned for feeling overwhelmed, like the least voluble character in the play itself, the stolid Anthony Dull, who, confronted with the observation that he has "spoken no word all this while," responds modestly, "Nor understood none neither, sir" (V.i.149–51). This flat-footed rejoinder is actually unwittingly trenchant, for much of the language of *Love's Labor's Lost* is not meant to be understood, at least in the sense that we understand words by seeing through them to their referents. What most of the male speakers in the play aim at is not clarity but cleverness and virtuosity, and language as a result tends to become performance rather than communication.

But a little patience with the dense language of *Love's Labor's Lost* will be amply repaid, for, if we can never quite recover the relish with which Shakespeare's original coterie audience presumably received the rich variety of verbal wit, we can at least come to recognize that this is a very funny play, and moreover that its difficulties, its sometimes bizarre peculiarities, are knowingly deployed by the playwright and not simply the by-products of a naive and immature style. Shakespeare here exerts a degree of open-eyed control over his material that quite exceeds anything in the three preceding comedies, and he seems in equal measure to point to the limits of the "great feast of languages" (V.i.37) his play serves up and to rejoice in "the anarchic spirit of liberation" that, as William C. Carroll has reminded us, is "the source of the play's vitality, its very heart."[19]

Having remarked that *Love's Labor's Lost* is a funny play, I must add that it is also a serious and curiously moving one, the notion of the incompatibility of these conditions being one of those prejudices that has led to the ignoring of, or (worse) condescension to, comedy in general. If it seems paradoxical or simply absurd to speak of this play's capacity to move, when its language is so thoroughly formal, stylized, and self-consciously artificial, consider that Shakespeare has given us abundant indication of why, at bottom, all characters, with the exception of the taciturn Dull, are afflicted with logorrhea and have abandoned themselves to the production of apparently endless discourse. Without for a minute losing sight of the fact that speech in a virtuoso variety of styles is for the people of *Love's Labor's Lost* (and most of the time, for us as well) joyously good fun, we may also note a certain defensive character in the garrulity, a repeated wish on the part of a speaker not merely to have his voice be heard, but to have his voice be the only one heard. And it is not only a matter of the ludicrous prescriptiveness of the low characters, of Armado's overbearing bluster in the verses with which he concludes his letter to Jaquenetta (IV.i.88–93), or Holofernes's pedantical objections to the way Armado pronounces the English language (V.i.17–26), or even the normally silent Dull's uncharacteristic insistence that the deer was a pricket (IV.ii.12, 20–21, 48–49). For we remember that the play begins with a kind of prescriptiveness as well, the restrictive oath founding the "academe" to which Navarre persuades his followers to subscribe.

The aspiration to control is evidently widespread in this play, at least among its male figures, and it extends to a broad spectrum of human experience, for it is a wish not only to control others, their behavior, their manners, even, in the case of Holofernes (one is slightly alarmed to learn he is a schoolmaster), the way they speak, but a wish to control the self as well, to make it invulnerable to assaults from within and without. "To war against your own affections / And the huge army of the world's desires" (I.i.9–10), as Navarre puts it in his opening speech, is no small part of the academic project he proposes. The asceticism of the academe amounts to a futile attempt to deny what is, after all, part of human nature and thus undeniable, though a maturer point of view might see its way to a sensible compromise with what the clown Costard aptly calls "the simplicity of man to hearken after the flesh" (I.i.217–18).

Considered in the broadest way this pervasive aspiration to control is nothing short of an attempt to deny death, to keep at bay the ravages of time, which at first seems an unimportant presence in this leisurely world, where everyone apparently has unlimited opportunity to converse, to play games, and to be clever. Perhaps only when the shadows begin to lengthen toward evening in the last scene, when the exploded Holofernes is cautioned about stumbling in the gathering darkness (V.ii.630), and, of course, when Marcade appears abruptly to announce the death of the king of France (V.ii.716), do we realize retrospectively that the clock has been ticking all along and remember that the very purpose of founding the academe in the first place has been to overcome "the disgrace of death" and spite "cormorant devouring Time" (I.i.3–4).[20] The shocking and, in effect, extrageneric entrance of death's ambassador, which does not so much conclude the play as bring it to a grinding halt, still has the power to surprise in performance even audiences otherwise familiar with the play through repeated readings.

There are perhaps reasons for this capacity to surprise and shock that go beyond the inherent grimness and the abrupt reversal of mood. For Marcade's sudden entrance toward the end of V.ii is but the last and broadest of a series of disruptions of various formal protocols that mark the lords' hesitant progression from the solipsism of the academe to the wooing games of the final sequence. There is first, of course, the founding oath itself, which is coming apart even as it is given, for while the lords are debating and swearing, Costard is being taken with a wench (in two senses, smitten by her and arrested in her presence) "in manner and form following" (I.i.205, again in two senses). The form of words that is the academic oath is remarkably ineffectual in controlling Costard's desires, or for that matter Armado's, who appears in the next scene despairing of his unwilling passion for "a base wench" (the same Jaquenetta who has been Costard's downfall) and casting doubt on Navarre's project of warring against affection:

> I will hereupon confess I am in love; and
> as it is base for a soldier to love, so am I
> in love with a base wench. If drawing my
> sword against the humor of affection would
> deliver me from the reprobate thought of it,

> I would take Desire prisoner, and ransom him
> to any French courtier for a new-devis'd cur'sy.
> I think scorn to sigh; methinks I should out-swear Cupid.
>
> (I.ii.57–64)

There is, further and famously, the series of overhearings and exposures in IV.iii, with Longaville exposing Dumaine and being exposed in his turn by Navarre, who is then exposed by Berowne, who has witnessed the whole sequence. But if Berowne feels "like a demigod" (IV.iii.77) as he surveys his infatuated colleagues, that is only because he is unaware of a context that encompasses him as well, one that will shortly assert itself when Costard and Jaquenetta enter (IV.iii.187) bearing Berowne's letter to Rosaline, earlier misdelivered by Costard to Jaquenetta and later redirected to the king of Navarre by Holofernes.

Evidently, forms in *Love's Labor's Lost* exist to be confounded, as the Princess anticipates the Pageant of the Nine Worthies will be: "Their form confounded makes most form in mirth, / When great things laboring perish in their birth" (V.ii.519–20). There is some slight irony at her expense, when later Marcade enters with the news that will confound the form that contains the Princess in her turn, no less a set of formal protocols than *Love's Labor's Lost* itself, a situation Berowne ruefully acknowledges: "Our wooing doth not end like an old play: / Jack hath not Gill. These ladies' courtesy / Might well have made our sport a comedy" (V.ii.874–76).[21] Shakespeare has contrived to make it seem that even those formal structures directly attributable to him, and not just to one or another of his characters, cannot permanently survive the gusts of passion and the ravages of time that experience brings with it. As in the later *Twelfth Night,* which *Love's Labor's Lost* interestingly resembles in a number of ways, a comic structure can keep out the wind and the rain only so long.

From this perspective of confounded forms we can begin to see something like a rationale for the effusive production of discourse that in one sense constitutes the sole activity of *Love's Labor's Lost.* For tedious as the obsession with verbal cleverness may occasionally become to a modern sensibility, we are still justified in seeing in it a reaction to the uncertainties of an unpredictable and uncontrollable world: the male characters of the play are so preoccupied with controlling language precisely because they cannot control experience. Mastery of language gives them the soothing illusion of being comfortably on top of things, verbal skill becomes a surrogate for the ultimately unattainable mastery of life and experience in general, and the result is a frequently magical and even fetishistic treatment of the word, as if in manipulating names we were also manipulating the things named. It is this magical shortcut that Moth is parodying when he tells Armado how he may study three years in an hour (I.ii.35–54)[22]; and Costard may or may not be parodying the same thing (it is often difficult to guess Costard's level of awareness) when he stumbles on an analogy between monetary and verbal inflation and decides always to use "remuneration" (Armado's pompous term for what we would now call a tip) in striking a bargain, on grounds that it sounds more impressive than "three farthings" and thus will increase their value in trade (III.i.136–42).

Children's play, we have been told repeatedly in recent years, is often an arena in which the child creates a scaled-down model of the world that he can manipulate with a facility unavailable to him in the real world.[23] Something analogous may be happening with the treatment of language in *Love's Labor's Lost,* a play particularly rich in the imagery of children's games and playthings, where characters treat words quite as if they were toys to be played with, as if they were simply there for the unproblematic delectation of the speaker. The attitude frequently results in a winning childlike quality, beautifully captured in Boyet's description of the lords' preparation for the Muscovite masque:

> One rubb'd his elbow thus, and fleer'd, and swore
> A better speech was never spoke before.
> Another, with his finger and his thumb,
> Cried, "*Via!* we will do't, come what will come."
> The third he caper'd, and cried, "All goes well."
> The fourth turn'd on the toe, and down he fell.
> With that they all did tumble on the ground,
> With such a zealous laughter, so profound,
> That in this spleen ridiculous appears,
> To check their folly, passion's solemn tears.
>                                         (V.ii.109–18)

There is here, to be sure, the unmistakable note of smug self-congratulation rather characteristic of the lords, but there is also that hyperactive exuberance so characteristic of children unselfconsciously enjoying themselves. And this may remind us of the pertinent distinction English speakers make between the "childish" and the "childlike," between self-indulgent behavior incompatible with full socialization and the innocent release of enthusiasm and energy.

Insofar as we understand Navarre and his followers as being childlike, we will also understand their verbal play as heralding and even furthering the development of mature relationships; insofar as we understand them as being childish, that same play will appear escapist, retrograde, and trivializing, something like an indefinite deferral of a responsible address to the world. Perhaps either possibility is at any moment present, which is one reason why we tend to experience the lords as rather deeper and more complex than their counterparts in the group that includes Armado, Holofernes, and Costard, although, Shakespeare being Shakespeare and committed to seeing all facets of any situation, even these characters have their fine moments in the face of the lords' ungenerous scorn in the final scene. And again, Shakespeare being Shakespeare, no distinction, including the one between the childlike and the childish, will ever be quite absolute, and even as the playwright directs our ridicule at the lords' folly, he makes us understand its source in the very real fears that young men on the verge of full manhood have about growing up, assuming responsibility, recognizing the inevitable erosions of time, and coming to terms with human mortality. The ultimate purpose of courtship and marriage is, after all, procreation, and in progeny one confronts the fact that one will be succeeded, the transience of one's personal tenure at the center of things.[24] How understandable, then, is the wish to remain in the paradise of childhood, and, like Cupid, whose servants the lords claim to be, achieve the status of immortal infant. But perhaps rather than being servants of Cupid, the lords would really prefer to be Cupid himself, the perpetually youthful god, who wounds all but is himself never wounded in turn.

The difficulty is that, no matter how sympathetic the fears that lead to regressive behavior, childishness is still just that. If it is simply impossible to turn your back on experience (and it is), the best course would seem to involve working out as graceful a compromise with experience as possible, one that recognizes the claims of others and makes concessions to them. It is this kind of mutuality and reciprocity that the ladies seem to aim at in all their converse with the lords, and their uncharacteristically rude action of turning their backs on the Muscovite masque and putting the precocious Moth hilariously out of his part (V.ii.158–74) may be a pointed way of indicating that the masque is another piece of rhetorical showing off, not something that requires face-to-face encounter because it does not seek dialogue. If the ladies render "no grace" to the lords' "penn'd speech" (V.ii.147), that may be because a penned speech cannot listen, it can only talk.[25]

*Love's Labor's Lost,* as has been frequently noted, is preoccupied with the problem of decorum, of what is fitting and proper, or, to use a term that also respects this play's concern for time and its passage, of what is seasonable. As Berowne aphoristically sums it up (and we remember that he is not always one to follow his own advice), "At Christmas I no more desire a rose / Than wish a snow in May's new-fangled shows; / But like of each thing that in season grows" (I.i.105–7). The sensibility of this play, for all its happy indulgence in verbal excess, finally runs against extravagance in any form, even the extravagance sometimes associated with protesting breaches of decorum, for it is perfectly possible in this preeminently dialecti- cal world to be excessive about insisting on moderation. And behaving ex- travagantly and out of season, or in a manner unbefitting one's time of life may best be thought of as an attempt to deny time, to deny that it matters or that one is subject to it. But all such attempts must prove, of course, illu- sory, as all must involve an unseemly shouting down of the opposition, a re- fusal to listen and respond. The irony is that in denying death in whatever displaced form, you become like it: rude, peremptory, not to be denied. As Holofernes says of Armado—in a signal instance of the pot calling the ket- tle black—"His humor is lofty, his discourse peremptory, his tongue filed, his eye ambitious, his gait majestical, and his general behavior vain, ridicu- lous, and thrasonical" (V.i.9–12). One of the reasons the demeanor of quiet and mutual exchange, "the converse of breath" (V.ii.735), is so valued in this play is that it is on the side of vitality and the fully social and human. There is no converse of death corresponding to the converse of breath. Death is finally inhuman because supremely discourteous and overbearing.

Holofernes's windy objection to Armado's inflated manner reminds us of a central strategy that the male characters of *Love's Labor's Lost* employ to deny the otherness of others and evade dialogue. The pedant's denunciation of the man who is otherwise so like himself amounts to a kind of scapegoat- ing, the technique of projecting one's own shortcomings on another and then anathematizing them. The phenomenon is far from uncommon in Shakespearean comedy (or, for that matter, in tragedy), but here it is par- ticularly widespread from the very beginning, as Navarre describes Armado as an amusing curiosity having no bearing on the lords and their own posturing:

> A man in all the world's new fashion planted,
> That hath a mint of phrases in his brain;
> One who the music of his own vain tongue
> Doth ravish like enchanting harmony.
>
> (I.i.164–67)

Between Holofernes's vehement criticism of the Spaniard and Navarre's gentler ridicule there is little to choose: both betray an utter lack of self-knowledge, and both remind us that the play is in one sense a series of such displacements of blame, from Armado's own declaration that Costard shall "be heavily punished" (I.ii.150) for an offense Armado himself is even now longing to commit, to Berowne's stepping forth "to whip hypocrisy" (IV.iii.149) in the complex overhearing scene, as he reprehends his colleagues for being in precisely the same state of infatuation as he finds himself. And the climax of all this evasion undoubtedly comes with the lords' ungenerous treatment of Costard and company in the final scene, which we are led to believe is directly related to the humiliating rout of the masquing Muscovites immediately preceding. As Berowne remarks to Navarre, who is wary of letting the pageant proceed, "We are shame-proof, my lord; and 'tis some policy / To have one show worse than the King's and his company" (V.ii.512–13). The lords' mocking response to the Worthies' pageant is simply their oblique way of taking revenge for their own dismal failure in a similar endeavor.[26]

As he would do again shortly with the play-within-the-play in *A Midsummer Night's Dream,* Shakespeare uses the Worthies' pageant in *Love's Labor's Lost* to focus certain of the play's central preoccupations, not the least of them its concern with mutual reciprocity in human relations. In a theater like Shakespeare's, relatively impoverished in technological refinement, where much is required of the audience in the way of active imagination, a production of a play before an audience may be likened to a conversation, a mutual giving and taking in a tolerant spirit of good will to the ultimate benefit of parties on both sides, off and on the stage. The lords' failure to grant theatrical premises, including the most fundamental aspect of the dramatic contract, the willingness to take actors as the characters they portray, suggests a want of generosity and self-confidence that will stand in the way of any very satisfactory romantic relationship, for it is nothing less than a refusal of the conversational principle. Holofernes, for once, puts the matter cogently: "This is not generous, not gentle, not humble" (V.ii.629).

Not humble indeed, and it can remind us not only of the lords' wooing according to the most fashionable conventions of Petrarchan love poetry, but also of how thoroughly Shakespeare, if not his characters, understood those conventions, as opposed to merely imitating them, and was able to exploit them as part of his meaning. For in spite of the Petrarchan lover's elaborate declarations of humility, his posture of prostrate adorer before the radiance of his beloved, he is in fact showing off, dancing pirouettes around a lady who in the typical sonnet sequence is not even granted a voice but is simply the merest occasion for the lover's verbal display. That this putative submission barely conceals self-congratulating smugness is perfectly revealed in Berowne's sonnet to Rosaline, where for all the deifying of the lady and abject promise of fealty to her, the author still finds the opportunity to pat himself on the back:

> If knowledge be the mark, to know thee shall suffice;
> Well learned is that tongue that well can thee commend,
> All ignorant that soul that sees thee without wonder;
> Which is to me some praise that I thy parts admire.
>                                                    (IV.ii.111–14)

It is altogether characteristic of Berowne at this stage that he manages to preen himself on his judiciousness and taste for the finer things in the midst of what purports to be self-forgetful praise of his beloved.[27]

Such failures of the conversational principle, the inability to respond to the true otherness of others, indicates the necessity of the year-and-a-day probationary period that the ladies impose on their suitors at the conclusion. And Berowne's probationary task, exercising his wit on the sick and dying, easily the harshest of the four tasks imposed, is nevertheless fitting for the man who has so evidently loved to hear himself talk. What Rosaline appropriately reminds him of is the reciprocity of speech, the give-and-take of conversation:

> A jest's prosperity lies in the ear
> Of him that hears it, never in the tongue
> Of him that makes it; then if sickly ears,
> Deaf'd with the clamors of their own dear groans,
> Will hear your idle scorns, continue then,
> And I will have you and that fault withal.
>                                                    (V.ii.861–66)

If moving "wild laughter in the throat of death" (V.ii.855) will prove an impossible task (and one suspects it will), then Berowne will learn something important about the limits of witty jesting, just as even now he is being brought to recognize the limits of other kinds of formal structures, including the play in which he is embedded. A year and a day are "too long for a play" (V.ii.878), as Berowne ruefully concedes, and once again form is confounded, this time by time itself.

If *Love's Labor's Lost* concludes on a rather chastened note, we should not conclude that it is therefore gloomy or pessimistic. Weddings are, after all, postponed, not cancelled, and the pair of exquisite songs, which conclude both the Worthies' pageant and the larger play in which it is contained, are in fact an achieved dialogue reminiscent of the medieval *conflictus* or *débat*, in which both sides of an issue are given a hearing and each is weighed against the other. If the cuckoo's call suggests the possibility of betrayal and infidelity in the midst of burgeoning love, the owl's merry note reminds us of the possibility of cheerfulness even in the dark of the year with its muddy roads and runny noses. The songs are a lovely vision of things in their season, and they offer the prospect at last of living in and with time rather than against it. The willingness to do that is perhaps this play's final measure of maturity.

## Chapter Three
# A Midsummer Night's Dream: Errant Eros and the Bottomless Dream

In the middle of the seventeenth century the diarist Samuel Pepys noted that *A Midsummer Night's Dream* was "the most insipid ridiculous play that ever I saw in my life."[1] Although this can hardly be taken as evidence of a unanimously held opinion or even of a consensus, it is probably a fair indication of the theatrical taste of Pepys's age, which favored the hard-edged, realistic milieu of London as the setting of comedy, rather than the exotic and fanciful places, the often outright never-never lands, in which Shakespeare preferred to set his comic plots. Restoration preferences may even reflect the ascendancy of Ben Jonson's literary stock, an author who took it upon himself in his comedies contemporary with Shakespeare's comedies and romances to censure the latter, sometimes rather harshly. As Jonson has a character say in the "Induction" to one of his most successful comedies, "[The author] is loth to make nature afraid in his plays, like those that beget Tales, Tempests, and such like drolleries, to mix his head with other men's heels, let the concupiscence of jigs and dances reign as strong as it will amongst you."[2] If "Tales" and "Tempests" sound like inescapable allusions to Shakespeare's *The Winter's Tale* and *The Tempest,* it is obvious that Jonson also felt the need to scold an audience that had recently embraced, apparently with considerable enthusiasm, "such like drolleries."

Jonson's strictures make it clear, among other things, that he disapproves of Shakespeare's apparent disregard for realism: making "nature afraid" can only refer to what Jonson understands metaphorically as nature's horror at the monstrous and fantastic features of Shakespearean comedy and romance. And yet a century and a half later we find the great Shakespearean critic Samuel Johnson saying in the "Preface" to his edition of Shakespeare's works, "Shakespeare is above all writers, at least above all modern writers, the poet of nature; the poet that holds up to his readers a faithful mirrour of manners and of life."[3] Clearly we have to do with very different ideas and as-

34

sumptions about what "nature" means, when one critic finds monstrosity everywhere and another "the genuine progeny of common humanity, such as the world will always supply, and observation will always find."[4]

The assumptions subtending this interesting contradiction are not at all easy to specify, and it is hardly my purpose in the present argument to attempt to do so. I will note, however, that any use of the term "nature" will involve anterior assumptions, and that to call something "natural" or "real" is emphatically not to place it beyond question or exempt it from discussion. The terms always beg a good many more questions than they answer, and for this very reason an examination of the problematics of the natural and the real lies at the heart of a great deal of Shakespeare's comic writing.

Perhaps Pepys's and even Ben Jonson's antipathy was based on what may seem to us now a serious misunderstanding of Shakespeare's attitude toward convention and the old stories and traditions he so often appropriated and remade in fashioning a play. If we assume, for example, that he simply took the conventions of fairy lore in *A Midsummer Night's Dream* at face value, that the play asks us to accept the existence of fairies as a natural fact for the duration of its action, then that play will very likely seem to us, in Pepys's words, "insipid" and "ridiculous," although such putative naïveté is precisely what recommended Shakespeare to many of his admirers in the high romantic period of the early nineteenth century. But our own century has become increasingly suspicious of a Shakespeare piping native woodnotes wild, that charming, if badly educated, primitive, whose "small Latin and less Greek" relieved him of the burdens of sophistication and delivered his audience from the vexatious inconvenience of having to think.[5]

It seems, in fact, far more productive and ultimately far more interesting to assume that Shakespeare handled fairy lore with a high degree of awareness that such material was precisely a cultural production, perhaps a matter of naive belief for some, but hardly inevitably so, either for himself or anyone else. That assumption renders the text of *A Midsummer Night's Dream* as neither Ben Jonson's monstrosity nor Pepys's insipid ridiculousness nor Samuel Johnson's nature but as metaphor, the "as if" figure of playful possibility:

> I am that merry wanderer of the night.
> I jest to Oberon and make him smile
> When I a fat and bean-fed horse beguile,
> Neighing in likeness of a filly foal;
> And sometime lurk I in a gossip's bowl,
> In very likeness of a roasted crab,

> And when she drinks, against her lips I bob,
> And on her withered dewlop pour the ale.
> The wisest aunt, telling the saddest tale,
> Sometime for three-foot stool mistaketh me;
> Then slip I from her bum, down topples she,
> And "tailor" cries, and falls into a cough.
>
> (II.i.43–54)

Puck's account of himself should forestall any very simpleminded conception of a Shakespeare who believed in fairies. Puck is in these lines so clearly a figure projected from the folk imagination, a way of giving a quasi-human identity to and thus providing a reason for a series of random domestic mishaps, the unseen or disguised power that we still sometimes feel to be behind a daily world experienced as perverse, or for unexplained reasons resistant to or thwarting of our purposes. In short, Puck is a metaphor given a body on the stage. When minor accidents occur, when everything seems to go wrong, when we are having, as we say, "a bad day," it is *as if* a mischievous sprite named Robin Goodfellow (and his last name, like a number of actions imputed to him, hints that he is not fundamentally opposed to human endeavor) were at work unseen. It might be said that Puck is the imagination's way of domesticating and ordering the random.

I shall have occasion to note that Puck may be seen as a good deal more even than this, for in addition to being part of the thematic content of *A Midsummer Night's Dream,* he is as well part of its dramatic technique, certainly an engine of the plot, but also, with Oberon, onstage audience to a spectacle he himself has set in motion. And, as the lines quoted above foreshadow, he is the chief supernatural agency for turning potentially tragic events into comedy, just as on the human level Peter Quince's amateur theatrical company manages to turn the tragic story of Pyramus and Thisbe into "very tragical mirth." It is surely significant that the hapless "aunt," who finds herself sitting on the floor to the amusement of all the company, including herself, has been in the process of "telling the saddest tale." Puck seems always to have some bearing on the generic status of occasions in which he intervenes, whether they are informal fireside gatherings or the kind of highly stylized courtly entertainment for which *A Midsummer Night's Dream* seems to have been originally designed.[6]

This movement from the level of thematic content to the level of formal structure seems in principle reversible; that is, as theme is formalized so too form is thematized, and it becomes difficult to assign any given element unambiguously to one category or the other.[7] But it is in virtue of the latter movement—from form to theme—that *A Midsummer Night's Dream* so often seems to turn on itself and its own workings, producing a meditation on its own status as a piece of theater and more largely on the institution of theater itself, its necessary conditions, and the role of its audience in establishing and maintaining those conditions. Such a high degree of reflexiveness is not altogether surprising in a play in which the bulk of the last act is devoted to a play-within-the-play, the theatrical representation of another theatrical representation, however uproariously inept and maladroit. Such reflexiveness will figure largely in the argument that follows, for being mindful of it is one of the surest ways of inoculating ourselves against the notion of Shakespeare the naif, the natural genius from Warwickshire, the untutored Bard whose pearls of wisdom are all the more valuable for being spontaneous.[8]

Such modes of self-awareness about literary conventions and about the theater itself lead inevitably to another issue we began to examine in looking earlier at *The Comedy of Errors*. It is undoubtedly a mistake to speak of any fictional character as if he or she were a real person, a procedure that is bound to lead, sooner or later, to various kinds of counterfactual argument, including the nineteenth-century mania for discussing the girlhood of Shakespeare's heroines, Lady Macbeth's children, and various details of the private life of the tragic hero before he steps on stage. Without for a minute wishing to detract from his undoubted achievement, I may instance the characterological analysis of A. C. Bradley as the culmination of this remarkable cult of personality concerning what are, finally, not personalities at all, but fictive constructs.[9]

Yet it is probably more tempting to commit this fallacy of character-as-personality when discussing Shakespeare's tragedies or histories than it is when discussing his comedies. Comic characters are already somewhat deprived of individuality by virtue of being so often based on types stemming from classical antiquity (e.g., the miles gloriosus or braggart soldier, the *senex iratus* or irrascible old man, the *servus* or tricky slave), and we thus frequently have the impression less of individual psychologies than of a set of roles, already in place prior to a particular play, being discharged in the given instance. Stage comedy as a genre is tailor-made to remind us of Aristotle's wisdom that in drama (though he is, of course, speaking of tragedies) role comes before character (*ethos*), and plot (*muthos*) comes before either.[10]

Shakespeare seems to be aware of these issues to the point where he exploits them for comic effect and dramatizes the process of an individual trying to assert himself and emerge from the web of language and tradition that is his defining matrix. Nowhere are Shakespeare's comic characters more typical than when they attempt this emergence, however, and nowhere are their speeches more replete with citations of the comic and romantic traditions in general than when they protest the absolute uniqueness of their feelings, for it just so happens that protestations about the uniqueness of love are one of the most conventional elements of romantic comedy. In declaring your uniqueness you end up sounding exactly like a veritable parade of other characters from the tradition, all of whom sound exactly like one another. In comedy the conventional will out, and there is little anyone can do to suppress it.

This paradoxical and often very funny effect of convention returning in the very act of repudiating it extends to plot, or plots, as well. If we think of the action of romantic comedy as the attempt on the part of a marginal and subject figure (typically a youth) to rewrite the plot of a central and authoritative figure (typically a father or ruler), then it is clear that in *A Midsummer Night's Dream* Lysander's scheme in the first scene to circumvent the will of Egeus (backed up by Theseus and the Athenian law concerning the father's right to dispose of his daughter as he sees fit) is an attempt to impose a plot or scenario more consistent with individual desire. And yet the lovers' flight from the tyrannical (and conventional) law of Athens delivers them all unwittingly into the power of another set of plotters, Oberon and Puck, who arrange, after some misfires, the happy ending traditionally associated with romantic comedy, a happy ending, we note, no less arbitrary than the strict law it displaces. The movement of the play is evidently not from tyranny to freedom, from the constraints of culture in Athens to the liberty of nature in the woods outside the city, but from one form of tyranny to another, the latter, perhaps, experienced as more benign and acceptable than the former, but still a tyranny in the sense of a determining convention nonetheless.

Here is a sample of the dialogue leading up to Lysander's disclosure of his scheme for fleeing Athens:

> *Lys.* Ay me! for aught that I could ever read,
> Could ever hear by tale or history,
> The course of true love never did run smooth;
> But either it was different in blood—
> *Her.* O cross! too high to be enthrall'd to low.
> *Lys.* Or else misgraffed in respect of years—
> *Her.* O spite! too old to be engag'd to young.

> *Lys.* Or else it stood upon the choice of friends—
> *Her.* O hell, to choose love by another's eyes!
>
> (I.i.132–40)

This remarkable little duet is not really calculated to make us sympathize deeply with lovers' travails, for it formally exemplifies in its artificial and stagey way the very constraint it otherwise protests. We may even suspect that these lovers are rather enjoying their plight, indulging themselves in their own sense of suffering and affliction. By the logic implied here, if the course of love were to run smoothly, then it would not be true love, and thus the lovers actually derive a sense of their own authenticity from the very obstacles that stand in their way. But this is not to make true love a unique emotion arising from the inner life of two unique individuals, but to assimilate it to a conventional pattern, to say that our particular love is true and unique precisely because it is like the love we read about in "tale or history"—an odd procedure at best for one supposedly asserting himself. We are given good cause to wonder about that free life Lysander envisions for himself and Hermia beyond the Athenian pale.

Undoubtedly the words to stress in Lysander's first speech in the passage above are "read," "tale," and "history." They mark out the specifically literary territory from which he draws his examples and remind us that in this instance we have a case not of art imitating life, but of life imitating art, during which process the human beings in question acquire precisely the typicality they otherwise reject. While believing that they are engaging in an action peculiar to themselves, Lysander and Hermia are actually acting out without realizing it an ancient repertoire of the behavior of literary lovers, repeated over the centuries by countless lovers in countless romances. And so saturated is the speech of the lovers in *A Midsummer Night's Dream* with the kind of language we associate with the romance tradition, so bound does their behavior seem by the codes of the same tradition (the resistance to paternal authority, the schemes to circumvent various "blocking characters," and the like)[11] that they may well come to seem the effects of that tradition and that language, rather than individual human beings initiating speech and action in their own right.

By this route we arrive at a view of dramatic character rather different from the one implied by Bradleian characterological analysis. For if comic characters are effects of a certain kind of language rather than individual people, we will be less tempted to probe their psyches and rather more drawn to investigating their interactions, the kinds of larger patterns they form, the sorts of poetic idioms they share, not the idiolects that insist on the

differences among them. Furthermore, we may notice that the principle of
interchangeability implicit in the diachronic comparison of Shakespeare's
lovers with other lovers in the comic and romance traditions is replicated
in the synchronic context of *A Midsummer Night's Dream*. Hermia and
Helena, Lysander and Demetrius are notoriously difficult to distinguish,
and even after an extraordinarily attentive reading we may experience some
difficulty in specifying just who has been smitten by whom at any given
stage in the action. This inability may not be altogether a weakness of readers but a genuine textual effect, deliberately planned and carefully fostered
by a Shakespeare determined to blur or erase all kinds of boundaries we normally take as given and natural, including the boundaries between one self
and another, or, to put the matter more broadly, between a self and an am-
biance that is partly made up of other selves. As Demetrius says of the
events of the night in the woods on the following morning (and a look at
IV.i.186–87 will confirm that it is indeed he!), "These things seem small
and undistinguishable, / Like far-off mountains turned into clouds."

So too may they seem to us, as we metaphorically awake at the end of a
play that Puck's epilogue invites us to treat as a dream (V.i.423–28). For
from several perspectives within the play we have been encouraged to see the
four young lovers not as personalities with distinguishing traits, but as counters occupying shifting positions in an elaborate game or dance, again, as
agents of an Aristotelian plot. There is, for instance, the gently ironic way
Puck greets the entrance of the lovers as they are rounded up and gathered
together at the end of the third act:

> Yet but three? Come one more;
> Two of both kinds makes up four.
> Here she comes, curst and sad.
> Cupid is a knavish lad,
> Thus to make poor females mad.
> (III.ii.437–41)

Puck's reference to the two sexes as "both kinds," as well as his calling the
women "females," tends to have a distancing and diminishing effect, to deny
what we like to think of as the dignifying distinction between human nature
and the rest of the animal kingdom. The effect is even stronger in his concluding lines:

> And the country proverb known,
> That every man should take his own,

> In your waking shall be shown.
> Jack shall have Jill;
> Nought shall go ill:
> The man shall have his mare again, and all shall be well.
>
> (458–63)

The generic names suggest that character has become something very close to mere "plot-fodder": all you need for a story of this sort is two of both kinds.[12]

It would be possible, though perhaps unnecessary, to multiply examples almost indefinitely. In general, however, we may notice that this principle of interchangeability, along with the transgression of boundaries normally thought of as secure, is supported by the play's preoccupation with meta-morphosis, with the idea of one person or thing changing into another person or thing.[13] Helena at the outset, in love with Demetrius, who scorns her in favor of Hermia, wishes she could change into Hermia in order to possess whatever mysterious and unspecifiable attractions the latter possesses:

> Sickness is catching; O, were favor so,
> Yours would I catch, fair Hermia, ere I go;
> My ear should catch your voice, my eye your eye,
> My tongue should catch your tongue's sweet melody.
> Were the world mine, Demetrius being bated,
> The rest I'll give to be to you translated.
> O, teach me how you look, and with what art
> You sway the motion of Demetrius' heart.
>
> (I.i.186–93)

And later on she will well and truly become Hermia in the sense that she will occupy Hermia's position in the wooing game, after Puck's initial mis-taking of Lysander for Demetrius and his partial attempt to set the mistak-ing right have brought it about that Helena herself is pursued by both men, and Hermia has become the odd woman out (III.ii).

The height of confusion in the wood is something like a mirror image of the configuration of lovers with which the play begins, for in the wood we have the two men who have previously been rivals for Hermia's affections suddenly competing with equal energy for Helena's.[14] And Helena's re-sponse to this vertiginous shift is altogether interesting, because it seems an instance of that imaginative habit of mind we looked at above in discussing Puck's status, a habit that attempts to project a certain stability into an ex-perience that is in fact utterly random and arbitrary:

> Can you not hate me, as I know you do,
> But you must join in souls to mock me too?
> If you were men, as men you are in show,
> You would not use a gentle lady so;
> To vow, and swear, and superpraise my parts,
> When I am sure you hate me with your hearts.
> You both are rivals, and love Hermia;
> And now both rivals, to mock Helena.
>
> (III.ii.149–56)

Faced with an otherwise inexplicable volte-face on the part of the men, Helena can only deny it by insisting that it is pretense, a particularly cruel prank, born of a sadism the implications of which would be rather disturbing, if it were indeed sadism. Nor does Helena's comically desperate assumption in this instance entirely circumvent the problem of the arbitrary, for the cruelty and hatred implicit in the prank, if it really were a prank, would be just as inexplicable and rationally unfounded as the love that the two men "truly" express. The arbitrary, like the conventional to which it is closely related, has a way of returning in the very attempt to dispel it.

I have already noted some of the ways in which character can be seen as an effect of language rather than the other way around, and I should note that the confusions in the wood and the interchangeability of characters there are the direct result of an impressive array of punning, figural, and antithetical uses of language—all contributing to a pervasive transgression of boundaries. The repeated use of the word "rivals" in antithetical senses in the last two lines from Hermia's speech quoted above (the men are rivals in the sense of "adversaries" when it is a question of Hermia's love, but rivals in the sense of "partners" when it is a question of mocking Helena) contributes to our sense of swiftly changing positions, and the convergence of opposite meanings in the same word suggests a sameness in what we otherwise think of as the greatest difference. Shakespeare is here exploiting a feature of Elizabethan English—where "rival" really could mean either "adversary" or "ally"—that he may elsewhere treat neutrally.[15]

Or consider further a remarkable rhetorical feature of the lovers' language, the speaker's pervasive reference to the self in the third person, using his or her own proper name. As Helena says, "And now both rivals, to mock Helena." Lysander will fall into the same mode a little later in this exchange:

> *Her.* But why unkindly didst thou leave me so?
> *Lys.* Why should he stay, whom love doth press to go?

> *Her.* What love could press Lysander from my side?
> *Lys.* Lysander's love, that would not let him bide—
> Fair Helena!
>
> (183–87)

The effect of this curious mode of self-reference, in which all the lovers in-dulge from time to time (and it extends to referring to a present interlocutor in the third person as well—"What love could press Lysander from my side?"), is in part designed to objectify the speaker and make him seem faintly ludicrous and operatic. It is as if those involved in the wooing confu-sions were at once both participants and spectators, in and out of the game simultaneously, watching, perhaps with a good deal of narcissistic relish, their own play. In short, they seem, as we often say without thinking about what we really mean, "beside themselves."

Shakespeare plays in *A Midsummer Night's Dream* with the word *prop-erty* or the idea it expresses in at least three senses. There is first the common sense of "possession," a sense which by virtue of Athenian law extends to people as well as things, the sense implied when Egeus calls Hermia "what is mine": "And she is mine, and all my right of her / I do estate upon Demetrius" (I.i.96–98). Second, there is the technical but still familiar sense of "stage property," various portable items used to create dramatic il-lusion. It is to these that Peter Quince refers when he says, "I will draw a bill of properties, such as our play wants" (I.ii.105–6). And there is finally the broader sense, everywhere implied, of those traits, elements, or qualities that make a person or thing uniquely what he or she or it is and not some-one or something else. It is in the latter sense that the lovers in the wood are "unpropertied," deprived of themselves or their individuality, made to seem interchangeable, although in another sense shared by the first two defini-tions they are also "propertied,"[16] that is, reduced to things as they are ma-nipulated by Oberon and Puck, a process that really begins in the first scene with Egeus's insistence on the notion of his daughter as his property. In ei-ther case, the sense of the personal in human beings is lost, very much in-cluding the sense of the personal in human desire. It becomes difficult to conceive of a desire for a particular person, when in principle one person seems interchangeable with another, and we may come to suspect that desire is finally ungrounded, not circumscribed by a particular object, not a want-ing of anyone or anything specifically, but just a wanting. Desire, we may begin to suspect, is like Bottom's dream, "because it hath no bottom" (IV.i.216).[17]

Nor will it really do to say that depersonalized desire is the effect of magic, an effect that will simply vanish when the lovers emerge from the wood once again into the world of daylight. This is simply to ignore the fact that the first wandering of desire takes place in Athens before the action of the play proper begins. We are told that Demetrius has transferred his affections from Helena to Hermia, and if we are not told why, it is either because there is no reason (desire is not only impersonal but arbitrary), or, what amounts to much the same thing, because Demetrius's desire for Hermia is an effect of Lysander's desire for her in the sense that Lysander's desire may seem to Demetrius to confer upon Hermia the status of the desirable.[18] This would simply be one more example of the phenomenon of interchangeability, of the principle that one's identity is always elsewhere, for Demetrius's desire in this case would not be intrinsic to him but would derive from another.

What follows is that we no more have to posit a Shakespeare who believed in magic than we had to posit a Shakespeare who believed in fairies. Magic too is finally a metaphor, and as the lovers fall under its power, they really submit to the metaphorical expression of desire's unpredictable volatility, its whimsical nature, its tendency to veer from object to object, refusing to be circumscribed by any particular object. This, far more than inflexible fathers and arbitrary laws, is the ultimate tyranny of *A Midsummer Night's Dream,* showing once again that the movement of the play is not best described as a passage from tyranny to freedom but as a passage from one expression of the tyrannical to another. And what we witness of the lovers in the wood must make us a little skeptical about the neat solution their final marriages impose. One of those marriages, after all, the one joining Demetrius with Helena, remains the effect of love-in-idleness, a case of enchantment that is not in principle immune to further disenchantments.

It may well seem that, given all the giddy confusion of the lovers' night in the wood, the doings of Peter Quince and his troupe of artisans-turned-actors provide a kind of ballast, a stable ground against which we view the figure of antic desire. What is done in the theatrical sense with the plot of the lovers is undone with the plot of Peter Quince and company, as these simple men set about casting, rehearsing, and finally performing *The most lamentable comedy and most cruel death of Pyramus and Thisbe.* And this process of flatfooted undoing extends even to such metadramatic matters as the "verbal scenery," which, given the virtually bare stage of the Elizabethan theater, along with a fluid and swiftly moving dramaturgy that precluded elaborate sets difficult to change, was Shakespeare's most important means of suggesting locale. In his drama in general speeches set the scene, and for the most part we accept the fact that a scene is located where the characters say it is located.

If we bear the device of verbal scenery in mind, we will notice that, among other things, Shakespeare uses the second act of *A Midsummer Night's Dream* to establish the sylvan setting. The two longish scenes that make up the act are both full of a lush language aimed at leading us to imagine a forest:

> I know a bank where the wild thyme blows,
> Where oxlips and the nodding violet grows,
> Quite over-canopied with luscious woodbine,
> With sweet musk-roses and with eglantine;
> There sleeps Titania sometime of the night.
>
> (II.i.249–53)

After more than 400 lines of such imagery we may well be prepared to accept the forest setting, but no sooner are we so prepared than Quince and company enter with an unwitting counterreminder:

> . . . and here's a marvail's convenient place
> for our rehearsal. This green plot shall be
> our stage, this hawthorn brake our tiring-
> house, and we will do it in action as we will
> do it before the Duke.
>
> (III.i.2–6)

We are made forcibly aware that what we have been looking at in the course of the preceding act is not a wood but a stage, and that what we have seen on it (and will continue to see) are actors.

The artisans are not the sort of characters that a dramatist less confident (and less playful) than Shakespeare would care to introduce. Their flat-footed literalness is dreadfully efficient in destroying whatever illusion the play has otherwise managed to produce and sustain, and we are justified in suspecting that the amateur troupe is, among other things, Shakespeare's wry way of calling attention to the fragility of illusion in *A Midsummer Night's Dream* or in any other drama. Given the radically limited technical means at his disposal, Shakespeare must have been constantly aware of the threadbare character of the theatrical enterprise, the bare stage, the men in women's parts, the paltry two or three hours allotted to enact a story that may actually have unfolded over decades. But his consistent response to this structural impoverishment seems not to have been to hush it up by any means, but to face it frankly and as far as possible exploit it, to draw it into the play itself, to thematize the very inconveniences that a lesser dramatist might try to suppress.

The homely artisans are thus a means of calling attention to the theatrical machinery of *A Midsummer Night's Dream* from the inside, and their earthiness and flashes of common sense provide a perspective from which the "aery nothing" of the lovers' fancies seems delusion merely. And yet in this exquisitely evenhanded play it is, of the mortals, Bottom, and Bottom alone, who, in return for an indignity he barely notices, actually sees a fairy, and not just any fairy but the Queen of Fairies herself. That we can choose to see this fact as evidence of Bottom's literal-mindedness (incapable himself of imagining a fairy, he must be shown one) *or* as evidence of the proverbial visionary powers of the simple and innocent, is itself evidence for the kinds of delicate poise Shakespeare's play so often achieves.[19]

Although all the artisans are driven by a thoroughly literal habit of mind, Bottom in particular seems completely impervious to illusions, metaphors, and metamorphoses (including the quite literal one that befalls him). His appetite for role-playing—the most obvious form of metamorphosis *A Midsummer Night's Dream* offers—appears to be boundless (in I.ii Bottom wants to play Pyramus, Thisbe, *and* the lion simultaneously!), and yet wherever he goes and whatever he becomes, he remains stolidly himself, unmoved by what otherwise seem the most astounding occurrences.[20] Even the Queen of Fairies' passion fails to unsettle him:

> *Tita.* I pray thee, gentle mortal, sing again.
> Mine ear is much enamored of thy note;
> So is mine eye enthralled to thy shape;
> And thy fair virtue's force (perforce) doth move me
> On the first view to say, to swear, I love thee.
> *Bot.* Methinks, mistress, you should have little
> reason for that. And yet, to say the truth,
> reason and love keep little company together
> now-a-days. The more the pity that some honest
> neighbors will not make them friends. Nay, I
> can gleek upon occasion.
> *Tita.* Thou art as wise as thou art beautiful.
> *Bot.* Not so, neither; but if I had wit enough
> to get out of this wood, I have enough to serve
> mine own turn.
>
> (III.i.137–51)

Doubtless much of the comic effect here derives from the fact that while Titania speaks in the ornate verse associated with the fairies, Bottom persists in using his serviceable and colloquial prose. He is neither startled, surprised, nor awed by the sudden apparition of the Fairy Queen declaring her passion, and, although he will go with Titania, for the moment he is undiverted from his project of finding his way out of the forest.

What is true for Bottom in the presence of the supernatural is equally true for Bottom in the presence of the theatrical, for he is never wholly "in" his part of Pyramus, anymore than his colleague Snug is wholly "in" his part of the lion. The altogether hilarious performance in the fifth act is indeed hilarious largely because of the amphibious effect of men half in and half out of the roles they attempt. No sooner has Bottom "died" as the Pyramus he has never really succeeded in becoming than he resurrects himself as the Bottom he has been all along:

> *The.* Moonshine and Lion are left to bury
> the dead.
> *Dem.* Ay, and Wall too.
> *Bot. Starting up.* No, I assure you, the
> wall is down that parted their fathers. Will
> it please you to see the epilogue, or to hear
> a Bergomask dance between two of our company?
> (V.i.348–54)

The performance is all the funnier, because the artisans so overestimate the effect of their bungled presentation that they utterly destroy the possibility of such illusion as it might have produced by employing wholly unnecessary devices like Snug's speech warning the ladies that he is not a real lion (V.i.219–26). Furthermore, while the artisans grossly overestimate the effect of their playing on the audience, they also grossly underestimate the ability and willingness of that audience to supply in imagination what the stage itself cannot supply. Thus, if a wall and moonlight are unavailable, they will be represented by human actors—a failed effect, which would have been much better produced by a few oral allusions to a wall and moonlight in the manner of verbal scene setting. What Peter Quince's company is unable to grasp is Samuel Johnson's pronouncement on the nature of dramatic illusion: "It is false, that any representation is mistaken for reality; that any dramatick fable in its materiality was ever credible, or, for a single moment was ever credited.[21]

Johnson is, as so often, right on the mark: we never experience people and events on the stage quite in the same way we experience them in daily life. To do so might in fact constitute a pathological response. We are always aware to some degree in the theater of the amphibious nature of people playing roles, partly in and partly out of the characters they enact. The colossal failure of the artisan's play is simply an extreme case of what is to a lesser degree an element of any theatrical production. What Johnson does not say, but what is clearly implied in his argument, is that it is only the audience's grasp of theatrical conventions and ultimately its goodwill in construing those conventions that save all plays from seeming trivial and jejune, in Hippolyta's words (and she sounds, as Anne Barton remarks, remarkably like Samuel Pepys pronouncing on *A Midsummer Night's Dream* as a whole) "the silliest stuff that ever I heard" (V.i.210).[22]

Theseus's response to Hippolyta's impatient stricture has to do with just this necessity for goodwill: "The best in this kind are but shadows; and the worst are no worse, if imagination amend them" (V.i.211–12). And Hippolyta's further rejoinder is perhaps true in a way that in her present mood she does not intend: "It must be your imagination then, and not theirs" (213–14). It must, indeed, in every instance of theatrical presentation be the audience's imagination that to some degree completes the drama, fills in the gaps, or simply ignores the inescapable limits of the spectacle. An Elizabethan play is a strictly reciprocal enterprise, something that takes place between performers and audience, the result of an active cooperation. The audience is implicated in the play in at least two senses, for not only is the play, as we say rather loosely, "about" experience, that is, it comments upon how we live and behave, but also the play is drawn into the audience (or the audience into the play) by virtue of the fact that we must be active and sympathetic participants, not passive observers merely. And, as we join this interesting symbiosis, we may gradually realize that the border between art and life is permeable, that it is not always possible to establish it with certainty, and that just as plays are often lifelike, so life is often playlike, histrionic, a matter of shifting roles and postures, rather than an array of stable essences. The courtly young men with their sophisticated wisecracks and witty criticisms of the artisans' seriously intended clowning, of course, do not know that just the previous night they themselves were in precisely the same relation to the observing fairies as the artisans are now in to the observing young men. But we know, and as we watch the courtly young men watching the artisans, we may come to the ironic awareness that they have recently enacted a play that Puck has called a "fond pageant" (III.ii.114), a play in its own way just as silly as the one currently unfolding.

Theseus too seems to forget this principle of the interchangeability of art and life, particularly in his great speech on lovers, madmen, and poets at the beginning of the final scene before the play-within-the-play commences. "I never may believe / These antic fables, nor these fairy toys," Theseus says of the lovers' tale about their night in the wood: "Lovers and madmen have such seething brains, / Such shaping fantasies, that apprehend / More than cool reason ever comprehends" (V.i.2–6). Here is an apparently unassailable distinction between imaginative apprehension and reasonable comprehension, and yet Theseus's comprehension may not be quite as comprehensive as he seems to believe. We have already seen that a fantastic figure like Puck can function as a way of understanding or at least of making sense, as a way of giving, as Theseus says of the poet's pen, "to aery nothing / A local habitation and a name" (16–17). We are all involved with the imagination to this degree, Theseus included. And Shakespeare makes wryly available to us an irony that cannot in the circumstances be available to Theseus. We may be reminded that this man who affects superiority to "antic fables" (and the word *antic* means both "grotesque" and "antique," that is, "ancient") is himself the product of a set of what are for us antic fables, the legends and myths of the heroic deeds of Theseus in company with the likes of Hercules and Pirithous.[23] These are in principle no more probable than fairy stories and enchantment or what must be the lovers' tangled account of their night in the woods, and if Theseus expects his courtly peers to believe them (and the evidence is that he does and they do), it is by no means clear why he cannot reciprocate by believing in the story of the events in the wood. One man's history, it would seem, is another man's antic fable. If Shakespeare is gently skeptical about fairy lore and magic in the thoroughly relativized world of *A Midsummer Night's Dream,* he seems equally skeptical of some of the ways we go about believing in what we perhaps too facilely call the "real" world.

Theseus too, like the lovers in the wood, is thus embedded in a literary matrix of which he is unaware, a fact the play slyly acknowledges by including as one item in the list of entertainments for the wedding night "'The Battle with the Centaurs, to be sung / By an Athenian eunuch to the harp'" (V.i.44–45). This is, of course, an allusion to the epic battle of the Lapithae, led by Theseus's friend Pirithous, against the Centaurs, who had attempted to carry off Pirithous's bride. Aided by Theseus, the Lapithae succeeded in driving the Centaurs from Thessaly. The Theseus of Shakespeare's play rejects the recitation of the battle on grounds that Hippolyta has already heard the story from his own lips ("We'll none of that: that have I told my love, / In glory of my kinsman Hercules" [46–47]). He claims himself as the original and consigns the proposed recitation to the status of a mere mimetic repetition. And yet we may well suspect that the opposite is the case, that the character is the effect of the legend, rather than the legend the effect of the character. Theseus's real origin is in the imagination of an Athenian singing to a harp, and he is thus no less a fictional construct than Oberon or Titania or Puck.

It would be a mistake, however, to adopt a smug position and assume that we in the offstage audience command the ultimate perspective and control all ironies. The complex situation that the play-within-the-play generates—an offstage audience watching an onstage audience watching a play—is calculated to raise the possibility of further regress, to tempt us to look over our shoulders and find that we in our turn are being watched, that we too are embedded in a social matrix we neither fully understand nor control, a matrix that speaks in us far more than we speak in it. We are all to an extent the effect of others, for we are always constrained by the expectations and interpretations of our fellows, a group that may be as restricted as those immediately behind us in the theater, watching us watching an onstage audience watching a play, or as dilated as the social and cultural contexts in which we must function. The self as self-determining entity, the play finally suggests, may be as much an illusion off the stage as it is on.

## Chapter Four
# The Merchant of Venice:
# Sources and Suppressions

The best evidence would seem to date *The Merchant of Venice* 1596 or early 1597, that is, a year or so after *A Midsummer Night's Dream* (1595–96) and before either *The Merry Wives of Windsor* (1597) or *Much Ado about Nothing* (1598–99). In spite of the features that connect it with these other comedies, its distinctive qualities are perfectly obvious. It anticipates in many ways those late comedies that have come to be called "problem plays," and the enduring problem the figure of Shylock in particular presents to analysis, although reminiscent of the problem posed by Malvolio in *Twelfth Night,* remains unresolved and perhaps unresolvable. Venice, after all, needs the moneylending Shylock in a much more urgent way than Illyria needs Malvolio, and yet for all Venice's need for Shylock, Venetians continue to oppose and revile him with a ferocity that contradicts the very Christian principles on which their opposition ostensibly rests. The sense of a thick social texture and the interlocking dependencies of a real money economy are never very far beneath the surface of *The Merchant of Venice,* no matter how refined and full of sensibility the rhetoric of some Christian Venetians. And it has seemed to many students of the play that the questions of law and justice that Shylock's ferocious bond has raised are merely swept aside in the final act rather than honestly addressed.

The sources of Shakespeare's Venetian comedy are somewhat uncertain. The first story told on the fourth day in Ser Giovanni Fiorentino's collection of tales *Il Pecorone* (first published in Italian in 1558) is close enough to Shakespeare's play to make it seem a major influence, even though no English translation appeared in Shakespeare's lifetime. There we find the young man in pursuit of a mysterious heiress, financially backed by his friend (and, according to Fiorentino, his godfather), a friend who has sealed to a bond that names a pound of flesh as a forfeit in lieu of interest. Shakespeare changed the process of winning the lady and a number of other details. Fiorentino's Lady of Belmont takes her suitors to bed and agrees to marry the one who can possess her sexually. She arranges to have them drugged, and when they inevitably fail the test, they forfeit all their property. Shakespeare chastened Fiorentino's rather racy version by substituting the test of the three caskets, which he may well have borrowed from the thirteenth-century collection of tales in Latin known as the *Gesta Romanorum,* although the motif is widespread in folktales and probably quite ancient.[1] In addition to a number of other possible sources, he may have been most directly indebted to a lost play entitled *The Jew,* which we know of only through a brief notice by the antitheatrical writer Stephen Gosson in his *Schoole of Abuse* (1578). It is probable that we will never discover precisely where Shakespeare gathered all the materials for *The Merchant of Venice* or how he fit them together.

But what is altogether certain is that, whatever the provenience of the materials that make up *The Merchant of Venice,* they are combined in a typically Shakespearean hybrid form. Portia's Belmont with its casket test straight out of folktale or fairytale is set against a far harder and more realistic Venice, recognizable as the great merchant republic at the height of its economic power, a cosmopolitan trading and financial empire chary of impugning the internal consistency of its laws, precisely because the credibility of the city in international markets depends on strict and impartial enforcement:

> The Duke cannot deny the course of law;
> For the commodity that strangers have
> With us in Venice, if it be denied,
> Will much impeach the justice of the state,
> Since that the trade and profit of the city
> Consisteth of all nations.
>
> (III.iii.26–31)

The merchant Antonio seems to seal his own grisly fate and offer himself a martyr to the strict justice on which the economic health of Venice undoubtedly depends.

Against the rigor of Venice Shakespeare set the graciousness of Belmont, the place of love and the source of the mercy that tempers justice in the play. At the center of Venice is Shylock, who declares, "I stand for judgment" (IV.i.103). At the center of Belmont is Portia, who declares no less straightforwardly, "I stand for sacrifice" (III.ii.57). Such clear-cut oppositions present a temptation to see the play in allegorical terms, as a contest between the Old Law and the New, with the New Law snatching a triumph from the jaws of defeat and finally fulfilling what it has vanquished.[2] There is doubtless some truth in such a reading, and yet to say that this is what the play is finally "about" seems unnecessarily reductive, for it sweeps away the ambiguities and uncertainties that give *The Merchant of Venice* its peculiar kind of fascination. We have seen, and will continue to see, how Shakespeare constructs two contrasting and apparently opposed worlds only to show how they interpenetrate and inform one another. No antithesis in the comedies is ever quite static; if we take it that *The Merchant of Venice* is in some sense about justice and mercy and the triumph of the latter over the former, a thoughtful reading may suggest that the case may be put the other way around: mercy must temper justice, but justice must continue to inform mercy, if the latter is not to become hopelessly sentimental and empty, the merest gesture, simply a part of the elaborate manner of the Venetian patrician. And to understand the play simply as a contest between the mighty opposites Portia and Shylock is, as we shall see, to ignore a rather subtler but just as insistently suggested contest between Portia and Antonio, a contest that lends itself more to a psychological reading than to an allegorical one. *The Merchant of Venice* continues to be a remarkably hardheaded, even realistic, play, in spite of its fairytale motifs and mysterious Belmont, right through the joyous celebrations of its fifth act.

It is also true that this play, as much as any other of the comedies and more than most, has provoked controversies of a high order.[3] The figure of Shylock, predictably enough, has been a focus of attention, and how we are to respond to him—whether as a simple stage villain, relentless opponent of the generous values of Christian Venice, or as an example of wronged humanity, the victim of Venetian callousness and its unexamined sense of natural superiority—continues to fuel a strenuous debate.[4] But debate has by no means confined itself to Shylock, and it is to another problem, no less central to our understanding of *The Merchant of Venice,* that I initially turn.

The play commences with what will prove to be a characteristic mystery about origins. The merchant of the title, Antonio, confesses to a feeling of melancholy (what we would now probably call depression) but is either unable or unwilling to account for the source of his feeling:

> In sooth, I know not why I am so sad;
> It wearies me, you say it wearies you;
> But how I caught it, found it, or came by it,
> What stuff 'tis made of, whereof it is born,
> I am to learn.
>
> (I.i.1–5)

For all Salerio's and Solanio's elaborate suggestions about Antonio's business worries, the question posed in the play's opening lines is never directly
answered. We are simply left to puzzle about it obliquely. As the scene un-
folds and the shifting group of characters narrows down to Antonio and
Bassanio alone in conversation, one kind of solution to the riddle of
Antonio's melancholy is suggested, if not directly asserted: Antonio's sadness stems from the thought of losing his dear friend Bassanio, who has already hinted at his plan to pursue a rich heiress of Belmont. It is certainly
significant in context that Antonio's first words to Bassanio show not only
his prior knowledge of his friend's plan, but also his urgent need to know
more: "Well, tell me now what lady is the same / To whom you swore a se-
cret pilgrimage, / That you to-day promis'd to tell me of?" (I.i.119–21).

This reading of the first scene has been and continues to be roundly denied. Lawrence Danson devotes an extended argument to demonstrating its
irrelevance and concludes that, although the loving friendship of Antonio
and Bassanio is a textual fact, the positing of competition between Antonio
and Portia "raises more problems of interpretation than it solves."[5] More recently Robert Ornstein has brusquely dismissed the notion of Antonio as a
"closet homosexual" and denied any hint of possessiveness in his attitude toward his friend.[6] And yet it seems altogether unnecessary to specify homo-
sexuality in the fullest and most literal sense on Antonio's part when one
can reasonably posit an attachment that probably has an erotic component
(as virtually all relations between human beings do), a kind of devotion and
bonding between members of the same sex characteristic of persons in certain cultures at certain stages of their personal development.[7] Helena of *A
Midsummer Night's Dream* invokes her relationship with Hermia as a re-
proach to what she takes to be Hermia's perfidy (III.ii.192–219), and we
shall see another Antonio, a minor character in *Twelfth Night,* whose devotion to Sebastian is set aside in favor of Sebastian's betrothal to Olivia.
Shakespeare continued to treat such youthful, monosexual attachments
right through the late romances, in the boyhood reminiscences of Leontes
and Polixenes in *The Winter's Tale,* for instance. There is rarely anything
queasy or sinister in such treatment, for Shakespeare seems to have accepted
the close attachment between members of the same sex as a normal stage in
the progress toward full adulthood and romantic heterosexual love. There
seems in principle no reason to rule out such an attachment between
Antonio and Bassanio in *The Merchant of Venice,* when the canon as a whole
provides numerous examples of the theme.[8]

If we bear in mind what seems to be Antonio's devotion to Bassanio,
much of the merchant's behavior reveals an interesting inconsistency and

conflict. Openhanded and spontaneous generosity is part of the patrician code of Venice, and the granting of loans without interest is a mark of the Christian gentleman—indeed, one of the most important things that distinguishes him from the Jew. This ethic helps to explain (though it hardly excuses) Antonio's haughty contempt for Shylock at their first meeting:

> Shylock, albeit I neither lend nor borrow
> By taking nor by giving of excess,
> Yet to supply the ripe wants of my friend,
> I'll break a custom.
>
> (I.iii.61–64)

This declaration of principle is striking because it is completely unnecessary; it seems, like much of Antonio's behavior, a histrionic and self-dramatizing gesture. In his aside at Antonio's entrance some lines before (41–52) Shylock has made it perfectly clear that he knows (and despises) Antonio's business ethics, and we are led to suspect that the merchant's supererogatory rehearsal of principle is not so much for Shylock's benefit as it is for Bassanio's. It is Antonio's way of communicating to his dear friend the extremes to which he is willing to go to serve that friend's interest.

Such self-dramatization is by no means confined to the third scene of the first act, and it is obliquely touched at the very outset. When Gratiano suggests that Antonio has "too much respect upon the world," Antonio's weary reply suggests a truth that perhaps even he is not entirely aware of: "I hold the world but as the world, Gratiano, / A stage, where every man must play a part, / And mine a sad one" (I.i.77–79). In deploying this familiar topos Antonio suggests on the face of it that melancholy is simply his assigned lot in life, a lot he accepts with patrician patience in the way the stage actor accepts and executes a script not of his own writing. And yet we may suspect that Antonio's part is active as well and has a rhetorical component, that it is designed at some level of consciousness to call Bassanio's attention to his sadness, and that it is to some degree chosen rather than imposed.[9] In this sense Gratiano's further joking accusation that Antonio's melancholy is an affectation aimed at gaining a reputation for profundity may strike a general truth, although the analysis of Antonio's specific motives is not entirely accurate:

> There are a sort of men whose visages
> Do cream and mantle like a standing pond,
> And do a willful stillness entertain,

With purpose to be dress'd in an opinion
Of wisdom, gravity, profound conceit,
As who should say, "I am Sir Oracle,
And when I ope my lips let no dog bark!"
(88–94)

And Gratiano's request of Antonio that he "fish not with this melancholy bait / For this fool gudgeon, this opinion" (101–2), may suggest that Antonio is, indeed, "fishing," if not for a reputation of gravity and wisdom, then at least for Bassanio's attention.

If we accept the interpretation that the first scene of *The Merchant of Venice* hints obliquely at Antonio's suppressed love for Bassanio and that his sadness has its source in the thought that Bassanio is on the verge of turning his attention elsewhere, much of Antonio's conspicuously self-dramatizing behavior becomes clear. There is, for instance, the matter of his exaggerated leave-taking on the occasion of Bassanio's departure for Belmont, as reported by Salerio in the second act:

"Slubber not business for my sake, Bassanio,
But stay the very riping of the time;
And for the Jew's bond which he hath of me,
Let it not enter in your mind of love.
Be merry, and employ your chiefest thoughts
To courtship, and such fair ostents of love
As shall conveniently become you there."
And even there, his eye being big with tears,
Turning his face, he put his hand behind him,
And with affection wondrous sensible
He wrung Bassanio's hand, and so they parted.
(II.viii.39–49)

Even in turning away, Antonio reveals himself as the very picture of an abandoned friend, and in so dramatizing himself there is little room to doubt that he seeks to ensure the very opposite of what he enjoins. In mentioning the Jew's bond he reminds Bassanio of who is underwriting the expedition to Belmont, and in telling Bassanio to forget him he actually reinforces a sense of profound indebtedness.

Antonio is the most vocal spokesman for the code governing the behavior of the Venetian patrician, that set of professed values that are at the heart of Venetian life and at the center of *The Merchant of Venice* as a whole. And yet, if we are alert to the motivation running beneath his expansive pronouncements, we may glimpse certain contradictions and suppressions implicit in that code, and we may come to feel that certain of its values are frequently invoked rather casually and very much taken for granted. Unstinting generosity both in spiritual and material matters is, of course, central to the patrician code to the point where generosity seems to be the secular equivalent of the Christian mercy which is Portia's initial watchword in the trial scene. The notion of the gift freely and spontaneously bestowed without thought of return informs Antonio's hatred of Shylock's usury, and his sense of business life as the heroic acceptance of risk and hazard explains his withering contempt for the sure returns Shylock arranges for himself. And yet this stringently realistic comedy seems to question whether such lofty ideals, unimpeachable in themselves, can ever remain completely pure as they operate in real relations between fallible human beings. It may be doubted that any gift is given between human beings without any thought of return in any form on the part of the giver or any sense of indebtedness on the part of the receiver.[10] In loftily condemning interest in the sense of "excess" or "usance," Antonio manages to hide the fact, even from himself, that he has made loans to Bassanio in return for a different kind of "interest," that is, the interest manifested as the attention and devotion of his friend. A suppressed or rejected fact of the money economy thus returns, as the suppressed or rejected has a way of doing in Shakespeare's plays, as a fact of an analogous spiritual economy no less central to human relations.

In presenting his generosity as unmotivated, a simple fact of his character that will not admit explanation, Antonio suppresses its origin in the wish for a return, for interest in the psychological or emotional sense. And this wish is in every way analogous to Shylock's far more openly expressed wish for interest of another kind, no matter how concerned the merchant is to establish differences and characterize the Jew as a kind of monster. Indeed, Shylock's very presence in Venice suggests a pattern of suppression that pervades Venetian life, for the play surely prompts the question of why he is tolerated at all, however savagely, if the patrician code so stringently rejects the institution of usury. If the Jew is really "the very devil incarnation" (II.ii.27–28), as the vulgar clown Launcelot Gobbo (as well as a disturbing number of his social superiors, including Antonio) characterizes him, why is he not thrust from the Venetians' midst? The answer can only be that merchant adventurers have need of the moneylender, however reticent their code about expressing this need. And for Shylock's part, we can be reasonably sure that he would not remain in Venice (to be kicked and spat upon by Christian patricians) were there any lack of customers for the service he offers.

Antonio's denials and the contradictions they engender are merely the central and clearest instance of Shakespeare's conception of Venetian society as a whole. For the Venice of the play is collectively engaged through its ideological self-representations in turning away from itself; it is composed of citizens concerned to deny or occlude the sources and foundations from which their collective life springs. Let us face one central matter squarely: for all the leisure and cultivated idleness among the Venetian citizens to whom we are introduced, for all the witty chat and bantering exchange so suggestive of a courtly aristocracy, and, perhaps most important, for all the sense of the bonds binding one human being to another as personal and emotional rather than economic, Venice is, to put the matter bluntly, a bourgeois capitalist republic based on trade and profit from economic exchange, the buying cheap of luxury items in one place and the selling of them dear in another. Venice has no landowning aristocracy and no underclass pledged by oath of fealty to the service of such an aristocracy. Its citizens are burghers, more or less prosperous according to the success or failure of their merchant ventures.

Several things follow from this bald recital of the economic facts. A social hierarchy based on the ownership of land, as W. H. Auden pointed out in a brilliant essay on *The Merchant of Venice,* is relatively stable.[11] As land is passed from one generation to the next within the family, social differences, who has power and who does not, remain secure. It may seem at first glance that the transition to capitalism sweeps away the notion of hierarchy entirely, that the putative equality of opportunity to venture and to gain or lose by venturing puts all on an equal footing. But a little reflection will reveal that societies always create differences between person and person. In a capitalistic republic like Shakespeare's Venice differences will be defined not according to who owns land and who does not, but according to who has accumulated a greater amount of money, who less. The point is that differences *will* be defined, one way or another. A brief look at the deference Salerio and Solanio accord Antonio in the first scene of *The Merchant of Venice* should dispel any notion that Venice is an egalitarian society. The crucial difference between Shakespeare's capitalistic Venice and a feudal aristocracy is simply that social hierarchy in the former has become unstable and unpredictable, a matter of whose luck has held, whose failed. It is not that capitalistic Venice has overcome the hierarchical principle, only that hierarchy has become a source of anxiety, for when the man currently at the top of the heap may be ruined by a stroke of impersonal fortune, who is to say who will be up, who down, tomorrow?

Wherever there is a permanent source of anxiety built into a society's structure, it is certain that there will also be ways, no less institutionalized and entrenched, for attempting to defend against it or ward it off. To such attempts we may refer the insistently idealizing tendency of Venetian rhetoric, its representation of the economy of Venice as a heroic enterprise wherein the hero-merchant repeatedly puts at risk everything he has in the hope of reaping profit in the end. But in this version the possibility of utter failure and loss is not really faced squarely, as is evident in Salerio's speech at the outset:

> I should not see the sandy hour-glass run
> But I should think of shallows and of flats,
> And see my wealthy *Andrew* dock'd in sand,
> Vailing her high top lower than her ribs
> To kiss her burial.
>
> (I.i.25–29)

Here the prospect of failure emerges as a stately and heroic spectacle, a tableau full of pathos that can hardly be grasped as the prelude to what we must otherwise understand as a loss of face and social position. And we may wonder further whether at a deeper level there is not some hint of competitive schadenfreude in Salerio's affecting representation of the foundering of one of Antonio's merchant ships.

If Venetian rhetoric is not to be taken quite as tendered but conceals both anxiety and tendentiousness, there is the further matter of the palpable contradiction in the merchant's attitude toward risk and venturing. For the merchant hedges his bets like any prudent businessman, or at least can say he does, for whatever reason, without provoking a ripple of surprise or objection.[12] Thus Antonio replies to Salerio's suggestion that he "Is sad to think upon his merchandise,"

> Believe me, no. I thank my fortune for it,
> My ventures are not in one bottom trusted,
> Nor to one place; nor is my whole estate
> Upon the fortune of this present year:
> Therefore my merchandise makes me not sad.
>
> (I.i.41–45)

Such prudence is not altogether different from Shylock's narrowly contractual dealings and seems of a piece with Antonio's astonishing indifference to the sinister implications of the moneylender's proffered bond in the next scene but one. Having there berated the Jew for trying to make "interest good" by adducing the story of Jacob and Laban ("This was a venture, sir, that Jacob serv'd for, / A thing not in his power to bring to pass, / But sway'd and fashion'd by the hand of heaven" [I.iii.91–93]), Antonio goes on to presume blandly on that same hand of heaven in reassuring Bassanio:

> Why, fear not, man, I will not forfeit it.
> Within these two months, that's a month before
> This bond expires, I do expect return
> Of thrice three times the value of this bond.
>
> (156–59)

It would be difficult to say why Antonio is so confident here, except that he is a Christian and therefore considers himself guaranteed the rewards of grace (a contradiction in terms), while Shylock the Jew (from the Christian perspective) must necessarily lose, just because he is a Jew.

Such an assumption, subtending as it seems to do the arrogant sanctimoniousness of Antonio's treatment of Shylock in the third scene, suggests some telling reasons for the vehement hatred with which Christian Venice as a whole regards the Jew. It is not only that Shylock's voice, refusing all the poetic mystification of Venetian rhetoric, provides an insistent and unwelcome reminder of the uncertainties inherent in the merchant enterprise, as when, for instance, he remarks to Bassanio that "ships are but boards, sailors but men" (I.iii.22). For Shylock's very Jewishness in a world where social definitions are always at risk and liable to shift seems to provide at least one difference that can be counted on, a difference that seems firmly a part of the order of things and as such invulnerable to the whims of an impersonal fortune. However his luck may run on the high seas and his place in the Venetian social order be affected accordingly, the merchant can always point to the one difference that never changes: he is a Christian and Shylock a Jew.

Antonio's deplorable treatment of Shylock in the third scene can thus be subsumed in the larger pattern of denial and repression that marks the Venetian social code and its anxious search for stable differences. And, as with any hyperbolic assertion of difference in Shakespearean comedy (like Touchstone's wry disquisition on court and country in *As You Like It*), we will inevitably suspect that the opposite obtains, that there is likeness in direct proportion to the energy with which difference is asserted. Portia's question, as she enters the Venetian courtroom as Balthazar (IV.i.174), is pertinent: "Which is the merchant here? and which the Jew?"

Portia herself, as we are now in a better position to see, is among the things that the Venetian social code represses. In reading or seeing *The Merchant of Venice,* it is impossible to overlook the fact that Venice itself is an overwhelmingly male world, a patriarchy indeed. Women apparently have no place whatever in the economic life of the city: they do not appear on the Rialto, nor are they even much mentioned, except as the subject of witticisms in dubious taste, as in the characteristically male banter exchanged by Salerio and Gratiano in II.vi. In Antonio's and Shylock's dispute about the meaning of the story of Jacob and Laban in Genesis 30 (I.iii.71–102) neither man mentions Jacob's pursuit of a wife. And it is certainly significant that the three women who actually do appear in the Venetian scenes, Portia, Nerissa, and Shylock's daughter, Jessica, only do so in public dressed as males, "obscur'd," to use Lorenzo's telling phrase, "Even in the lovely garnish of a boy" (II.vi.43, 45). It is as if for Christian and Jew alike in Venice human generativity were so entirely devoted to multiplying wealth that the generativity associated with sexuality and procreation has been almost forgotten.

But only almost, for the play as a whole remembers what Venice has tried to forget. It has often been remarked that the first two scenes of *The Merchant of Venice* draw Antonio and Portia in parallel: the first scene begins with the merchant announcing his mysterious melancholy that "wearies" him and his friends, the second with Portia's similar complaint that her "little body is a-weary of this great world." We can now see that Antonio stands in relation to Portia as represser to repressed, as the representative of the "great world" that excludes the feminine or admits it only in the form of a possession to be passed from the hands of one male to another. In the exchange with Nerissa in I.ii Portia's speeches are eloquent of her frustration, of her need to take action in a world that has cast her in a passive role:

> If to do were as easy as to know what were
> good to do, chapels had been churches, and poor
> men's cottages princes' palaces. . . . But this reasoning is
> not in the fashion to choose me a husband.
> O me, the word choose! I may neither choose who I would,
> nor refuse who I dislike; so is the will of a living
> daughter curb'd by the will of a dead father. Is it not
> hard, Nerissa, that I cannot choose one, nor
> refuse none?
>
> (12–14, 21–26)

The wish to be doing, to be acting rather than acted upon, will be fully sat-
isfied only when Portia enters the Venetian courtroom in the trial scene.
Meanwhile, her sphere of action vis-à-vis her suitors is restricted to the imaginative order, to the series of witty caricatures she offers in response to
Nerissa's question about her affections. Belmont seems at the outset not
only a fictional world, but a world in which activity is limited to the creation
of and confrontation with further fictions.[13]

One of the components of Portia's great vitality, which audiences inevitably respond to even when they are unable to articulate the source of their response, is the sense of abundant, if restrained, self-assertion implied in her
language throughout the process of her courtship. For all the enervation of
her opening lines, she is no confirmed melancholic like Antonio, out of
touch with crucial aspects of her feelings, but an energetic young woman determined to explore the possibilities within the restrictions imposed on her
by the will of a dead father. With the heroic Morocco and the pompous
Arragon she is polite if impersonally abstract, confining her remarks largely
to the conditions of the casket test. With Bassanio she is obviously ebul-
lient, unable to maintain the pose of impartial referee under the pressure of
intense feeling:

> Beshrow your eyes,
> They have o'erlook'd me and divided me:
> One half of me is yours, the other half yours—
> Mine own, I would say; but if mine, then yours,
> And so all yours.
>
> (III.ii.14–18)

In relation to Bassanio, these lines suggest an upwelling of feeling that masters her, and yet, in relation to her father, they equally suggest that Portia
has a will of her own, a choice, even though that choice may well be overridden by the outcome of the impending test.

Here, as elsewhere in *The Merchant of Venice,* Shakespeare introduces remarkable play with the ideas of possessing and being possessed, expressed
in the passage above in the rapid shift and substitution of possessive pro-
nouns: "yours," "mine own," "if mine, then yours." Portia seems to hesitate
between total self-possession and total submission, as Bassanio's eyes divide
her in reflecting a double image of herself. Such division may express the
plight of the female object under the gaze of the male subject, which seeks
to engross and possess the female entirely. But Portia's image of self-division
also anticipates the final scene of the play, where having divided herself by

her own choice between the roles of Portia and Balthazar and emerged victorious, she turns the image of ocular reflection around, so that now it is her gaze that overlooks and divides Bassanio, revealing his double allegiance, his loyalty divided between herself and Antonio:

> Mark you but that!
> In both my eyes he doubly sees himself,
> In each eye, one. Swear by your double self,
> And there's an oath of credit.
>
> (V.i.243–46)

The immediate point is that under the apparently effusive and spontaneous rhetoric of self-bestowal in the casket scene we are justified in seeing Portia's reservation of a part of herself, her wish for the kind of reciprocity and exchange in love that Antonio's unstinting but basically possessive generosity seeks to repress.[14]

This is, of course, one of the great problems with Antonio's generosity, that in giving without condition he tries to forestall restitution and thus to reduce his beneficiary to a state of permanent indebtedness, a process that Harry Berger calls, in a trenchant reconsideration of the casket scene, "mercifixion."[15] Berger convincingly demonstrates the ambivalence of Portia's speeches, especially of the phrase "I stand for sacrifice" (III.ii.57), as Bassanio prepares to make his choice. The sense is particularly ambiguous coming at the culmination of Portia's comparison of Bassanio to Hercules, herself to Hesione, the tribute offered by her father Laomedon to a sea monster in compensation for his refusal to pay Poseidon his wages for his assistance in building the walls of Troy. The overt terms of the comparison liken Bassanio to Hercules (55), the savior of Hesione, but are calculated to remind us that Hercules was motivated not by love for Hesione, but by the wish to possess Laomedon's horses, the promised reward for success. That Hesione herself was included as part of this larger bargain suggests Portia's fear of falling victim to male Venetian acquisitiveness quite as much as it does her admiration for Bassanio as a hero. Indeed, in Belmont as in Venice the heroic character of Venetian enterprise is still entangled with more mundane considerations of psychology and motive, with real social relations involving questions of dominance and submission.

It is all too easy to forget in the romantic world of Belmont that the legend of Hercules and Hesione itself is deeply involved with contracts and subsequent reneging, with broken faith and the abuse of bargains. Laomedon had reneged in the matter of Poseidon's wages, but the story goes on to tell us that he broke faith again in refusing to give Hercules his horses and his daughter in return for ridding Troy of the necessity of tribute. For all the obvious celebration of venture and risk in III.ii, the story is still shadowed by Laomedon's repeated refusal of reciprocity, for Laomedon is a father who thinks he can have it all his own way, who will not be accountable to his promises, and who can thus take without the necessity of giving in return.

This specter of the dominant father dogs the suitor who comes to replace him as well. Bassanio has repeatedly been accused of fortune hunting in his pursuit of Portia, and if the charge proves ultimately unfounded, it may nevertheless be understood as a response to an undeniable potential in Bassanio's "venture" to Belmont:

> Nor is the wide world ignorant of her worth,
> For the four winds blow in from every coast
> Renowned suitors, and her sunny locks
> Hang on her temples like a golden fleece,
> Which makes her seat of Belmont Colchis' strond,
> And many Jasons come in quest of her.
> O my Antonio, had I but the means
> To hold a rival place with one of them,
> I have a mind presages me such thrift
> That I should questionless be fortunate!
>
> (I.i.167–76)

"Worth," "thrift," "fortunate": it is not that such terms have no extended senses beyond the purely material, but that they surely begin in the material, as Shylock constantly reminds us, and that it is the sheerest sentimentality to pretend that they do not or to pass too lightly to the extended spiritual meanings of which they are capable. The quest for material gain remains a disruptive possibility in Bassanio's wooing of Portia, just as surely as his attachment to Antonio does.

It is with this in mind that we may begin to hear in the language of the casket scene certain voices that cut across or qualify the exuberant rhetoric of male heroic conquest and feminine submission, those elements that make Bassanio's romantic venture purely an extension of the myth of Venetian heroic merchant venturing. Portia's hyperbolic and apparently unqualified surrender to Bassanio is particularly suggestive in this regard:

> But the full sum of me
> Is sum of something; which, to term in gross,
> Is an unlesson'd girl, unschool'd, unpractic'd,
> Happy in this, she is not yet so old
> But she may learn; happier than this,
> She is not bred so dull but she can learn;
> Happiest of all, is that her gentle spirit
> Commits itself to yours to be directed,
> As from her lord, her governor, her king.
>
> (III.ii.157–65)

It is scarcely possible not to hear in Portia's phrase "sum of something" the homophonic "some of something."[16] Sum/some: the phrase hovers between "sum total," the whole, and "some," the part or fraction of that whole, just as "full sum" in the preceding line may suggest "fulsome," the overblown or swollen (cf. Shylock's "fulsome ewes" in I.iii.86), and thus the hyperbolic character of Portia's rhetoric. And if "lord," "governor," and "king" are undoubtedly submissive terms in context, we do well to remember that Bassanio's acceptance of Portia's ring (and we may hear the rhyming of "king" and "ring" even over the run of six lines) commits him to something other than absolute dominion. The ring, in fact, in its very circularity, stands for a reciprocal contract, an assertion of Portia's rights in Bassanio as well as his rights in her:

> This house, these servants, and this same myself
> Are yours—my lord's!—I give them with this ring,
> Which when you part from, lose, or give away,
> Let it presage the ruin of your love,
> And be my vantage to exclaim on you.
>
> (170–74)

There is, in short, in Portia's effusive self-bestowal nevertheless a note of wariness and reserve, a note amplified and borne out in the last two acts, where Bassanio's love and commitment will be on trial not once, but twice, first in the Venetian courtroom, finally in the reunion of lovers in Belmont. That Bassanio, as well as Antonio and Shylock, is, indeed, on trial in the fourth act is a fact likely to escape notice in an allegorizing view of the play that sees Portia and Shylock as the central antagonists. And yet Antonio's habit of intense self-dramatization and Bassanio's no less fervent response to it seem designed to notify us of an implicit contest for Bassanio's affection and of his profoundly divided loyalty so unacceptable in a mature romantic relationship. How can it well be otherwise, we may ask, when Bassanio's profession of loyalty to Antonio produces such a tart rejoinder from Portia-Balthazar:

> *Bass.* Antonio, I am married to a wife
> Which is as dear to me as life itself,
> But life itself, my wife, and all the world,
> Are not with me esteem'd above thy life.
> I would lose all, ay, sacrifice them all
> Here to this devil, to deliver you.
> *Por.* Your wife would give you little thanks for that
> If she were by to hear you make the offer.
>
> (IV.i.282–89)

Portia's task in the concluding acts is thus not single but threefold, and its three parts are closely implicated in one another. She must, to be sure, extricate Antonio from the toils of Shylock's legalism. But this is not only a Christian duty, for it includes releasing Bassanio from Antonio's claim upon him also, a claim that might well, with Antonio's death, involve Bassanio in endless mourning and memorialization. As Antonio declares in the courtroom, "You cannot better be employ'd, Bassanio, / Than to live still and write my epitaph" (IV.i.117–18). And finally, in freeing Antonio from Shylock and Bassanio from Antonio, Portia must take and assert the measure of her own autonomy among the male bonds of Venetian society; she must choose the self-division initially imposed upon her by Bassanio's male gaze (III.ii.14–18) and make it creative and self-creating. By becoming both man and woman in the disguise of Balthazar Portia attains presence in Venice and the status of effective agent.

But it is once again an indication of the realism of *The Merchant of Venice* that Portia's effective autonomy is not given at the outset, as perhaps Rosalind's is in *As You Like It*. The drama of the last two acts of the play is largely based on the heroine's growth, on the process of feeling her way toward a solution to the deadlock that both Shylock's intransigence and Antonio's histrionic devotion pose. It is a solution, as the play makes clear, by no means available to Portia from the beginning of the crisis. She begins, in fact, rather naively by proposing to buy out the problem ("What, no more? / Pay him six thousand, and deface the bond" [III.ii.298–99]); and once in the courtroom as Balthazar she embarks upon an interesting false start:

> *Por.* Then must the Jew be merciful.
> *Shy.* On what compulsion must I? tell me that.
> *Por.* The quality of mercy is not strain'd. . . .
>
> (IV.i.182–84)

This brief exchange is telling, far more so, in fact, than the famous speech on mercy that follows. For it is Portia, not Shylock, who introduces the idea of compulsion ("Then *must* the Jew be merciful"), yet she goes on to lecture Shylock on the properties of mercy, quite as if he had introduced the notion of compulsion and were pertinaciously insisting on it. There is a certain smugness in Portia's tone that is familiar enough, for it is precisely Antonio's tone in dealing with Shylock in I.iii. The current exchange recapitulates in little the whole mechanism of Venetian anti-Semitism: make by projection all that is contradictory or unacceptable in your own attitude a property of the Other and then anathematize it. This convenient maneuver has the great virtue of affording the Christian the opportunity to display the right attitudes and slogans while preserving their antitheses inviolate in himself.

But Portia's way is finally not Antonio's, and herein lies the key to her success. Where Antonio can only continue to present himself as a martyr to Shylock's legalism and thus to the principle of law in general, Portia, instead of obstinately insisting on the differences between Jew and Christian, law and mercy, submits herself to Shylock and his point of view with even more rigor than Shylock himself.[17] Her humility vis-à-vis the bond, her submission of herself to the literal character of the contract, to what it says and, more important, to what it does not say, is in one sense and despite her disguise an act of perfect feminine submission that nonetheless results in mastery. It is in daring to take Shylock's point of view, precisely in risking the similarities of Jew and Christian, that Portia succeeds in transcending them.

In presenting Portia as a character in process Shakespeare avoided the obvious sentimentality of presenting her as a saint. And if the final treatment of Shylock, especially his forced conversion, seems harsh and anything but merciful, it is at least the result of the literal logic he himself has invoked. What would compound our discomfort and make it intolerable would be the simple sweeping away of Shylockian rigor in the celebrations of the concluding act, a finale that has seemed to many students of *The Merchant of Venice* pleasant enough, but superfluous to the play's central concerns. But Portia is scarcely a repressor of sources in the manner of the Venetian gentleman, and it is no small measure of her triumph in the fifth' act that she manages to transfer some of the rigor of Venetian business dealings to the sphere of love in Belmont. In giving the ring to the "doctor" (and at

Antonio's importuning [IV.i.449–51]) Bassanio has undoubtedly reneged on a contract fully as solemn and binding as any commercial agreement made at Venice. In confronting Bassanio with his lapse, no matter how playfully, Portia asserts her own status not as some ancillary acquisition to be ignored when the male community is in crisis, but as a fully autonomous self to whom the same faith and reciprocity are due as are owing one merchant to another in a business transaction. And, as in any business transaction, there is a penalty for failure; faithlessness will be met with faithlessness[18]:

> Lie not a night from home. Watch me like Argus;
> If you do not, if I be left alone,
> Now by mine honor, which is yet mine own,
> I'll have that doctor for my bedfellow.
> (V.i.230–33)

Portia holds Bassanio finally accountable to his actions in a way Antonio with his sentimental generosity has denied doing, although, as we have seen, he has made implicit demands of Bassanio as stringent as Portia's explicit ones, a fact he seems to allude to with a rueful remark: "I am th' unhappy subject of these quarrels" (V.i.238).

*The Merchant of Venice,* it must be admitted, leaves us with the impression that Antonio is likely to remain unhappy, precisely because the quarrels of which he has been the unhappy subject have been resolved. What has been gained for female autonomy and reciprocal rights in the romantic relationships has been gained at the expense of the bonding between males characteristic of Venetian society. No one will doubt that some such gain for one aspect of life at the expense of another is at the very heart of romantic comedy, which is typically concerned with the growth of its protagonists into mature heterosexual relationships. Portia's besting of Shylock in the fourth act implies and prefigures her besting of Antonio in the fifth. In effecting this double exclusion she reveals what has been the case all along: that she is the ultimate source not only of wealth but of life itself, the mother in whom all men, however they go about to repress the fact, find their origin. As Antonio says upon reading of his restored fortunes in the letter Portia presents him (the source of which, incidentally, she leaves shrouded in mystery), "Sweet lady, you have given me life and living" (V.i.286). His remark implies a surrender to a principle succinctly stated by one of Shakespeare's later and happier comic protagonists, the Benedick of *Much Ado about Nothing:* "No, the world must be peopled" (II.iii.242).

# Chapter Five
# *The Merry Wives of Windsor* and *Much Ado about Nothing*

In 1702 John Dennis, the mediocre English dramatist and fair-to-middling literary critic, asserted in an epistle affixed to *The Comical Gallant* that *The Merry Wives of Windsor,* of which Dennis's play is a rewriting, was written at the command of Queen Elizabeth, who was so eager to see it "that she commanded it to be finished in fourteen days." The authority on which Dennis made this assertion remains thoroughly mysterious. He may have simply been trying to provide a rationale for his own revision on grounds that the original was hasty work requiring correction. But his remark, however motivated, appears to have founded a tradition, for we soon discover Nicholas Rowe in his edition of Shakespeare's works (1709) confirming the royal command and now adding that the queen was so well pleased with Falstaff as he appears in the two parts of *Henry IV* that she commanded the playwright "to shew him in Love." The next year the execrable dramatist Charles Gildon repeated the expanded story, telling the reader he is "very well assured" that Shakespeare completed his play "in a Fortnight." Again, the source of Gildon's assurance is scarcely clear: it may simply rest on the testimony of John Dennis and Nicholas Rowe.[1]

The tradition of a royal command, resting on no evidence whatever, has been remarkably persistent, and in certain quarters has even come to be accepted uncritically. But if Elizabeth really did want to see Falstaff in love, she must have been disappointed in the event, for the fat knight of *The Merry Wives of Windsor* is both lustful (though there are hints of his impotence) and venal, but he is hardly what anyone would call enamored. Nevertheless, the suspicion that this play was an occasional piece, if not written at the queen's command then at least commissioned for a court occasion at which her presence was likely, has remained a part of serious scholarly speculation. Indeed, a somewhat tentative agreement fixing the play's date in 1597 rests partly on Leslie Hotson's hypothesis that the nominal patron of Shakespeare's company, George Carey, Lord Hunsdon, the queen's lord chamberlain, commissioned the play as a way of thanking the queen for his elevation to the Order of the Garter in that year. Certainly some specific lines in the final scene mentioning not only the garter itself but the motto of its order (V,v.55–73) strongly suggest a connection with an occasion pertinent to its ceremonies.[2]

A date of 1597 and an occasion fixed by Hotson as the Garter Feast held 23 April at Windsor preclude neither a royal command nor a royal wish to see Falstaff in love, though they do nothing to support the case for either one. The date does, however, make strong the possibility that Shakespeare wrote *The Merry Wives of Windsor* between the first part of his *Henry IV* and the completion of the second part. The relation between the two history plays and the one comedy in which Falstaff appears has been much debated, but it is scarcely necessary to rehearse the debate here. Perhaps the most common sentiment has been disappointment, a sense that the Falstaff of *The Merry Wives of Windsor,* when compared to the complex rogue of the history plays, is a thing diminished in all but physical bulk.[3] And beyond Falstaff, there is the recurrence of what are scarcely more than names from the history plays: Falstaff's followers, Bardolph, Pistol, and Nym; his old acquaintance Justice Shallow, on whose property he has committed trespasses; and finally Mistress Quickly, erstwhile hostess of the Boar's Head Tavern in Eastcheap, who has somehow been translated to Windsor in the employ of the French physician Caius. Very little light is added by Page's brief objection to young Fenton's having "kept company with the wild Prince and Poins" (III.ii.72–73), apparently a reference to Prince Hal, which would place the action of the play in the reign of Henry IV, when it otherwise seems firmly fixed in the contemporary reign of Elizabeth. All things considered, it seems wiser to take *The Merry Wives of Windsor* on its own modest merits, rather than to compare it to the histories or to try to argue that the histories and the comedy somehow form a coherent whole.

But even among the comedies this play is an anomaly. While we have come to think quite rightly of Shakespearean comedy as being concerned with romantic wooing and winning, *The Merry Wives of Windsor* alone deals with married life in a settled community,[4] the stable, middle-class existence of an actual village, which, unlike the usual Shakespearean comic setting, must have been well known to most members of the original audience. Indeed, this play is nearly akin to contemporary "citizen comedy," and easily the most exotic thing about its Windsor setting is the presence of the Welsh parson Evans and the French physician Caius; but these two professionals have been so completely integrated into village life that, in spite of the outrages they commit on the English language, they have much the same status as any native Windsorite. They both have a certain professional stature, and the parson, at any rate, readily falls in with the rest of the villagers to counter the threat Falstaff poses to the stability of community life. It is significantly only Pistol, himself an unassimilated outsider, who stridently calls attention to Evans's exotic origin with the insulting epithet "mountain-foreigner" (I.i.161). The insult says far more about Pistol's alienation than Evans's.

Indeed, differences of social class are far more emphatic in this play than differences of national origin. Page does not merely express an idiosyncratic antipathy when he objects to Fenton's aristocratic connections, for the ordinary citizen's mistrust of the superior classes, the gentry and aristocracy alike, is never far from the surface, and, if Falstaff is any indication, it is well founded. The fat knight is the very embodiment of gentlemanly predation, the sexual and economic opportunism of a decaying leisure class, which rests on a conviction of natural right and thus has a clear conscience about exploiting those who have accumulated property through their own efforts.

But just here we may remark a certain problem that is not really resolved by play's end. For if Shakespeare clearly wished to celebrate the independence and integrity of the middle class in *The Merry Wives of Windsor,* he just as clearly did not wish to issue a blanket condemnation of the upper classes (particularly if the play really was a response to the queen's express wish). The assembling nobility at Windsor Castle hard by had to be accommodated within the comic harmony, and the gentry had to be shown as harmless and right-willed, if at times a trifle vain and self-important. The former Shakespeare rather cursorily included by means of the speech in the final scene alluding to Windsor Castle and the Order of the Garter (V.v.55–73); the latter he represented in the person of Justice Robert Shallow, whose mild pomposity and self-importance are absurd but scarcely exclude him from the good feeling of the Windsor community. And by making this gentleman, as well as ordinary citizens, the victim of upper-class predation, Shakespeare was trying to suggest the fundamental innocence of the higher reaches of society, even as he was suggesting their decadence through the figure of Falstaff. Finally, Fenton, to whose aristocratic connections and high birth Page so strenuously objects, is made to confess initial pecuniary motives in wooing Anne Page (thus justifying to some degree her father's opposition) even as he renounces them in declaring his pure love for the young woman (III.iv.13–18). His conversion enables the union of a gentleman with an ordinary citizen that is virtually the emblem of the comically harmonized society at the end.[5]

Clearly, Falstaff is made to bear the onus of whatever criticism Shakespeare wished to aim at the upper classes, and in this rather limited sense perhaps we can see the knight as a ritual scapegoat, taking upon himself the sins shared by a large group of people. But as far as the citizens of Windsor are concerned, it is difficult to see in Falstaff's punishments any very profound ritual content, as if some magical procedure for purifying the village on the threshold of a new year were taking place.[6] If we were to experience the real psychological depth of scapegoating, we would have to understand the Windsor wives as casting out in Falstaff illicit desires that they themselves harbor, as we understand Antonio in *The Merchant of Venice* to reprove in Shylock faults that are just as common among Antonio's fellow Christians. But nothing seems further from the case in *The Merry Wives of Windsor*. The fidelity of Mistresses Ford and Page is absolute, unquestioned, and unproblematic, a given that the play asks us simply to accept. Indeed, in another kind of play Ford's insane jealousy might well have the effect of driving his wife to the transgressions of which he obsessively suspects her, on the principle that she has already paid the price for infidelity and might as well enjoy the fruits. But in this play Ford's jealousies only confirm his wife in her determination to remain faithful. The fact seems to be that *The Merry Wives of Windsor* does not have the degree of interiority that would render any ritual content thematic.

Certainly none of this should be taken as disparaging the play, only as cautioning against making of it something that it is not. This rather slender comedy does indeed show Shakespeare's skill in plotting and his fecund linguistic gifts, but it seems futile to claim for it the same depth and interest that we find in work like *A Midsummer Night's Dream, The Merchant of Venice,* or *Much Ado about Nothing.* And few readers of the two parts of *Henry IV* will find in the Falstaff of *The Merry Wives of Windsor* anything like the dazzling wit and brilliant evasions of the figure who goes by the same name in the history plays. The Falstaff of the comedy seems at times a mean-spirited bully, arrogant and presumptuous, but never an inspired jester, the man in the history plays who can stir an issue to its depths with an apparently simple pun. Such entertainments as *The Merry Wives of Windsor* does contain should speak for themselves without inflationary claims about profundity.[7]

With *Much Ado about Nothing,* thought to date from 1598 or 1599, we return to the familiar comic pattern of wooing and winning, of young love triumphing over the killjoy spirit, of the contention between the generations, with the added and very considerable attraction of the war between the sexes as well, brilliantly embodied in the phosphorescently witty Beatrice and Benedick. This couple are apparently Shakespeare's invention, no possible source seeming directly pertinent to the story in which they figure, and it is easy to forget, so engaging are they, that their relations form the subplot of *Much Ado about Nothing,* a companion piece to the far more conventional story of Hero and Claudio. The main plot is a version of a familiar story involving a calumniated maiden, and, as such, could derive from a number of sources, Ariosto's *Orlando Furioso,* Spenser's *The Faerie Queene,* and Bandello's *Novelle* prominent among them. In another kind of characteristic graft, reminiscent of *The Taming of the Shrew* and its contrasting heroines, Kate and her sister Bianca, Shakespeare has joined a thoroughly conventional romantic plot with an idiosyncratic and far more realistic story, and the complex interaction that results is but one mark of the great sophistication of this play, which exerted an influence on English drama throughout the seventeenth century and beyond.[8]

The title of this brilliant comedy shares with the title of *As You Like It* and the subtitle of *Twelfth Night; or, What You Will* an ironic suggestion of inconsequence, as if what we were about to see were merely an entertaining trifle with so little integrity of its own that it can be made to mean anything we like, or in the present case, simply a tempest in a teapot. There is, to be sure, much ado about nothing in *Much Ado about Nothing,* from the scandal surrounding Hero based on Don John's slander, to the Watch's energetic pursuit of Deformed, a nonexistent character conjured from an overheard and misunderstood remark of the drunken Borachio (III.iii.124ff.) and progressively elaborated as Deformed continues (not surprisingly) to elude capture. And yet a certain homophonic pun, first noted by the eighteenth-century editor Lewis Theobald and remarked by a succession of commentators, can alert us to this play's substantial concerns. It seems that in Shakespeare's English "nothing" was pronounced very like "noting," that is, marking or taking note, and thus the play dramatizes much ado about no less a crucial topic than the way we go about interpreting and understanding the world and one another, what sort of assumptions we make about the constant flow of information, true and false, that experience provides.[9]

That most of the action of *Much Ado about Nothing* turns on false or erroneous noting and marking, deceptions, misprisions, and mistakings of various kinds is apparent from the outset. Much of the first act and the long first scene of the second are devoted to setting up Claudio's mistaken impression that Don Pedro, who has undertaken to be Claudio's proxy in the wooing of Hero, has betrayed this trust and is in pursuit of Hero for himself. That the mistake is fostered by the treacherous Don John turns the incident into a kind of prologue to the far more consequential duping of Claudio in the concluding acts, as well as producing serious misgivings in us about Claudio's easy gullibility, an alacrity in believing the worst about people that does not altogether redound to the credit of this rather bland and superficial comic hero. The incident leads no further in any direct sense, and it is a measure of Shakespeare's apparent eagerness to establish a climate of mistakings and erroneous assumptions that, quite contrary to his usual practice, he here devoted the whole opening movement of a play to an episode that, whatever its value in establishing theme, has no further consequences as far as the plot is concerned.[10]

Given a world so likely to generate error and misconception, it is altogether striking that the putatively sophisticated gentlemen of *Much Ado about Nothing* tend to take noting in the sense of interpreting very much for granted. As in *The Merchant of Venice,* there is evidently a patrician code of conduct in force in this comedy, and a central part of it is the imperative to a kind of hearty openness and expansiveness, a free and easy way of taking the world and its people on the terms offered without reservation or skepticism. A crucial assumption about the transparency of signs is evident from the outset in Leonato's observation concerning the tears Claudio's uncle has shed on receiving the news of his nephew's honorable actions: "There are no faces truer than those that are so wash'd" (I.i.26–27). The remark is innocent enough, and we certainly have no reason to doubt the sincerity of Claudio's uncle, about whom, in any case, we hear nothing further. But it may occur to us in retrospect, after an accumulation of deceptions and mistakings, that tears, as any crocodile knows, are a sign and, as such, may be used to tell lies. Contrary to Leonato's pronouncement, it may be that there are no faces more false than those washed with tears.

As long as this aspect of patrician demeanor remains a formula governing the relations between men we may experience it as harmless and even generous. The hearty affection that appears to obtain between Leonato and Don Pedro, for instance, is at best attractive and at worst no worse than the kind of hyperbolic offering and response characteristic of those with unlimited leisure and resources at their disposal. As Don Pedro says of Leonato's hospitality, "I tell him we shall stay here at the least a month, and he heartily prays some occasion may detain us longer. I dare swear he is no hypocrite, but prays from his heart" (I.i.148–52). But at times in *Much Ado about Nothing* the patrician assumption that the world is simply and unproblematically there, available for taking up without reflection or interpretation, indicates not so much a generous openness as, on the one hand, a potentially destructive naïveté, and, on the other, a tendentious arrogance that is anything but the spontaneous, free and easy address to the world it would seem. We will not be far from the mark if we see the patrician openness and apparent generosity as a form of hyperbole, an overassertion marking its opposite. For to say that the world is unproblematic and available to me without a certain amount of strenuous interpretation is to say that I control it, and such an assertion may be a defense against the nagging feeling that I do nothing of the kind. And from this perspective, openness to a world that is assumed to be open to me really depends on a covert fix. True openness is constituted by the willingness to accept the other on its own terms, but here I am agreeing to be open to the world only so long as that world agrees to remain what I say it is.

The disillusioned sentimentalist, as Shakespeare well knew, often turns nasty. When the world finally refuses his patronizing pat on the head and proves more complex than he has allowed, he feels his judgment impugned, his assumptions exposed, and his honor compromised. This may help to explain, though it will never excuse, what many have experienced as the shockingly cruel behavior on the part of both Claudio and Don Pedro on discovering, as they believe, the degenerate behavior of Hero.[11] The lady whom Claudio has called "a jewel" (I.i.181), and of whom Don Pedro has averred on no particular grounds save his good opinion of his own discerning, "That she is worthy, I know" (I.i.229), suddenly seems to escape the control of the men's romantic clichés and vapid Petrarchan idolatry. But the disillusioned sentimentalist is hardly cured of sentimentality, he merely veers to the opposite extreme, no less sentimental and simplistic, and from believing women to be pure and innocent, suddenly thinks he has discovered that they are all perfidious and corrupt:

> Farewell,
> Thou pure impiety and impious purity!
> For thee I'll lock up all the gates of love,
> And on my eyelids shall conjecture hang,
> To turn all beauty into thoughts of harm,
> And never shall it more be gracious.
> (IV.i.103–8)

The sentimentalist still thinks he has the world well weighed up and thus under control. But he has merely traded one reductive paradigm for another.

It is striking that with the speech quoted above the romantically gallant Claudio has come to occupy just the position of the earlier Benedick, the wit who thinks, before he too succumbs to romance, that universal cynicism is the same thing as profundity and penetrating insight:

> That a woman conceiv'd me, I thank her;
> that she brought me up, I likewise give her most
> humble thanks; but that I will have a rechate
> winded in my forehead, or hang my bugle in an
> invisible baldrick, all women shall pardon me.
> Because I will not do them the wrong to mistrust
> any, I will do myself the right to trust none;
> and the fine is (for the which I may go the finer),
> I will live a bachelor.
>
> (I.i.238–46)

And with both men we are reminded how nearly they resemble the bastard Don John, how Benedick's brand of merry misogyny in particular may slide over into rooted and saturnine churlishness. Don John is far more than an agent of the plot in *Much Ado about Nothing* (though he is certainly that too), for he defines the darkest potential in some of the characteristically male attitudes in this play.

Central to those attitudes, and quite contrary to the gallantry and courtliness of the patrician code, there is evidently a deeply founded mistrust not only of Hero specifically but of women in general. It will not escape even a casual reader of *Much Ado about Nothing* that the perennial Elizabethan joke about cuckolds, the reference to the invisible horns said to adorn the brow of those husbands whose wives have been unfaithful to them, is repeated with something like obsessive regularity. From Leonato's nervous joke in the first scene about his paternity (I.i.105) to Benedick's parting advice to Don Pedro to marry because there "is no staff more reverent than one tipp'd with horn" (V.iv.122–24) we are treated to a string of rueful references to women's faithlessness and the inevitability of betrayal when men place their trust in them. It is clearly a subject never far from the minds of these otherwise confident and self-assured men, who present themselves so conspicuously as being in charge of themselves and those who depend on them.

References to cuckoldry and marital infidelity in Shakespeare's work are by no means confined to *Much Ado about Nothing,* for they pervade the entire canon. We have just seen something of the lengths Ford's insane suspicions of his wife drive him to in *The Merry Wives of Windsor.* But one of the most revealing references to cuckoldry also happens to be the last, occurring in the long expository second scene of *The Tempest,* as Prospero expounds the past to his daughter, Miranda. As he reveals the unexpected truth that he has been a powerful prince in days gone by, Miranda, wide-eyed and scarcely believing her ears, asks quite naturally, "Sir, are not you my father?" It is a moment that calls for nothing more than quiet reassurance, and so it is striking that Prospero chooses to introduce the topic of paternity: "Thy mother was a piece of virtue, and / She *said* thou wast my daughter" (*The Tempest*, I.ii.55–57; emphasis added). We can scarcely pass this off as formulaic banter, particularly when we remember that Prospero is a powerful magician, who otherwise enjoys a reputation for omniscience, but who apparently is as helpless as any other man when it comes to determining paternity with any certainty. That the husband really is the father of those he is pleased to call his children remains a matter of faith and trust even for those with supernatural endowments.

It would seem, then, that in at least one crucial area of experience the men in *Much Ado about Nothing* are not really in charge, and this because, as Freud was fond of pointing out, motherhood is always certain, fatherhood never. "Maternity," he remarked in a famous passage, "is proved by the evidence of the senses while paternity is a hypothesis, based on an inference and a premiss."[12] And it would further seem that the openness implied by the patrician code, the notion that everything is what it seems and that what people are is immediately and unproblematically available, is a defense against the uncomfortable realization that in the crucial areas of human relations nothing has this kind of simple certainty. And again, when this defense falls victim to what Claudio and Don Pedro assume to be the irrefragable evidence of their senses, their response is not to posit the estate of women (like the estate of men) as morally mixed, fallible but scarcely irredeemable, but to jump to the extreme and opposite conviction, which we may well feel to have subtended their dealings with women all along, that because not all women are demonstrably pure and saintly, then they all must be corrupt and perfidious.[13] In either case the men are saving the appearance of their sovereignty by positing as fully knowable and therefore manageable an area of experience that can only rest not on certain knowledge but on trust and mutual goodwill.

The man's unwelcome discovery that his precious honor lies substantially in the power of the woman he otherwise believes he controls is certainly an unsettling blow to his amour propre, and it has the further effect of introducing him to the notion of ambivalence, to the fact that human feelings, like many chemical elements, rarely occur in their pure form, but are always compounded with other feelings, not infrequently with their opposing trends, as joy often coexists with sadness, love with hatred. It is man's fate in Shakespeare's romantic worlds to desire what threatens him, to stake his identity on that which bodes its loss, and this paradoxical state of affairs seems bound to generate a certain complexity of feeling. The rather shallow gallantry of Claudio and Don Pedro may be a defense against this troubling complexity; it has in any case led them to posit a reductive model of the emotions, where one is either simply in love with a woman (standing for all women) who is a saint, or in headlong retreat from a woman (equally standing for all women) who is an abandoned whore.

"'Tis once, thou lovest," Don Pedro says in response to Claudio's declaration (I.i.318), as if any feeling were, in good positivist fashion, a simple fact. In one sense, of course, the remark simply follows the conventional protocol of the kind of romantic story from which Shakespeare derived the main plot of *Much Ado about Nothing,* the kind of story in which falling in love is an unproblematic transition and all obstacles on the way to the consummation of that love are uniformly of an external kind. But it is rarely Shakespeare's way simply to adopt a convention uncritically. He rather places it, takes a stand toward it, with the result that in the current instance it is not so much that the main plot seems constructed in obedience to conventional protocol as that the characters in that plot behave *as if* it were. It is not really Shakespeare, so it appears, but Claudio and Don Pedro who project a romantic scenario so reductive that it seems bound to come apart when faced with the complexities of genuine feeling.

No small part of Shakespeare's strategy in problematizing the conventions of his main plot is his inclusion of the parallel subplot, which reflects and refracts the main action in a variety of ways. And it is not simply a matter of literary patterns and inert juxtapositions inviting the audience to see comparisons and contrasts, for the plot actively reads the subplot and reads it wrong, its people constantly offer interpretations that seem framed to flatter the interpreter rather than genuinely responding to an other. A little reflection reveals that the conspirators against Beatrice and Benedick read this couple in exactly the way they read themselves—as unproblematic, one-dimensional creatures. To the likes of Don Pedro, the constant exchange of barbed comments between Beatrice and Benedick simply reveals an antipathy that it will be the conspirators' mighty task to turn to attraction. As Don Pedro says in his characteristically self-assured manner,

> I will in the interim undertake one of Hercules'
> labors, which is, to bring Signior Benedick and
> the Lady Beatrice into a mountain of affection
> th' one with th' other. I would fain have it a
> a match, and I doubt not but to fashion it, if

> you three will but minister such assistance as I
> shall give you direction.
>
>                                   (II.i.364-70)

Surely the accomplishment of "one of Hercules' labors" appeals to Don Pedro because it will redound to his credit as an organizer and flatter his sense of being in control. But our own reading of Beatrice and Benedick may be at odds with Don Pedro's, and where he sees a man and a woman whose indifference he will convert into "a mountain of affection" by means of his great efforts, we may see a man and woman protesting too much their mutual indifference, energetically resisting, and all the while bearing witness to the current of affection that is already present at the outset of the play. It is often remarked that Beatrice's insulting inquiries about Benedick in the first scene show at the very least an active interest that is, whatever its complexion, scarcely compatible with indifference.[14] And for his own part, Benedick has a tendency to reject suggestions that no one has made. "I would not marry her, though she were endow'd with all that Adam had left him before he transgress'd" (II.i.250-52), he hyperbolically protests after Beatrice has insulted him at the ball, as if everyone had been tiresomely urging this course upon him. And a few lines later, as Beatrice enters, he waxes positively prolix:

> Will your Grace command me any service
> to the world's end? I will go on the slightest
> arrand now to the Antipodes that you can devise
> to send me on; I will fetch you a toothpicker
> now from the furthest inch of Asia, bring you the
> length of Prester John's foot, fetch you a hair
> off the great Cham's beard, do you an embassage to
> the Pigmies, rather than hold three words' conference
> with this harpy. You have no employment for me?
>
>                                   (II.i.263-71)

So Benedick announces, at what seems unnecessary length, his unwillingness to remain in Beatrice's company; but if her presence is truly distasteful to him, he is perfectly free to leave quietly. Like a later marcher to a different drummer, Jaques in *As You Like It*, Benedick does not want to leave so much as he wants to be seen leaving—a very different matter indeed.

What we experience in both Beatrice and Benedick, then, is not so much disdain as the spectacular enactment of disdain—again, a very different matter. And it is the sense of the simultaneous presence of opposing trends in this witty pair, in contrast to the violent shuttling back and forth between extremes characteristic of the men of the main plot, that gives them a sense of depth and complexity together with a poignancy that seems beyond the scope of the limited emotional repertoire of the conventional Don Pedro and his fellow conspirators. Indeed, wit is at the heart of the matter, for, so far from being the sign of the absence of feeling, wittiness is best thought of as a sign of its presence, the subject's way of controlling or denying feeling, a means of warding off the vulnerability that a straightforward confession of affection, for instance, might generate. As Benedick says to Don Pedro and Claudio, using a pun that makes his remark altogether pertinent to himself, "The body of your discourse is sometime guarded with fragments" (I.i.285–86). A guarded wariness is the hallmark of both Beatrice and Benedick in their relations with one another.

That the people of the main plot misread the people of the subplot to the point of taking them as they proffer and perhaps even understand themselves is a bold stroke of technique on Shakespeare's part: by arranging to have the play internalize a misreading of itself he anticipates and forestalls a similar misreading on the part of the audience. He calls our attention to nuanced complexity by making those on stage oblivious to it, so that by the time Don Pedro and Leonato have repeatedly mentioned Beatrice's merriness, for instance, we may well have come to suspect the copresence of some rather profound melancholy as well, the dark side of merriness, as loneliness is the dark side of independence. We may detect something poignant in this woman whose thoughts of the single life lead her spontaneously to thoughts of death, as she imagines herself fulfilling the proverbial fate of old maids and leading apes into hell, then ascending to heaven and living with the bachelors "as merry as the day is long" (II.i.39–49). Somehow it does not seem all that merry, but the mixed quality is utterly lost on Leonato. As he says to Don Pedro of Beatrice,

> There's little of the melancholy element in
> her, my lord. She is never sad but when she sleeps,
> and not ever sad then; for I have heard my daughter
> say, she hath often dreamt of unhappiness, and wak'd
> herself with laughing.
>
> (II.i.342–46)

Some 50 years ago, the Shakespearean editor George Lyman Kittredge, apparently in an attempt to rationalize Beatrice's laughter in this situation, glossed "unhappiness" as "some amusing roguery or other."[15] This gloss admirably supports Leonato's view of the matter, but it misses the suggestion that laughter can be defensive. We may rather be curious about why Beatrice dreams of unhappiness in the ordinary sense at all, and why she must repress that unhappiness with laughter.

As far as the representation of complexity and depth of character is concerned, the main plot of *Much Ado about Nothing* may actually seem supplemental to the subplot, an effective technical device for supporting a representation that belongs, to be sure, to the subplot but has often been experienced as the central one of the play. But we must bear in mind that the relationship between the two plots can be made to work the other way, and that the subplot has the technical effect of calling in question the conventions on which the main plot otherwise seems unproblematically based. As we have already seen, it is not so much that the main plot is a conventional story as that the people it contains behave as if it were, guiding their actions and forming their opinions according to fashionable standards, all the while believing that they are acting with commendable independence.[16] The men of the main plot, to use one of Dogberry's inspired blunders (IV.ii.67), are firmly "opinion'd" by the powerfully influential, if largely unspoken, norms of the elegant world they inhabit. This means, among other things, that we cannot dismiss Claudio's abrupt loss of faith in Hero as merely the kind of thing that happens in conventional stories: it may be a conventional response, one altogether characteristic of young men of Claudio's social position who find themselves in his situation, but it does not follow that the story in which it occurs is itself uncritically conventional. And if we have grasped the antithetical logic of the relationship between Beatrice and Benedick and have come to think that their sudden falling in love in response to what is, after all, minimal prompting suggests an affectionate trend always and already present beneath the explicit persiflage and witty insult, we will also begin to suspect that beneath the romantic treacle of Claudio's wooing runs a contrary trend of mistrust, fear, and even hatred of the woman who always has the power (whether or not she has the will) to shame him in the eyes of his cronies. Claudio's violent rejection of Hero, in short, is made to seem no more the creation of Don John's rather clumsily melodramatic practice than the sudden love of Beatrice and Benedick is made to seem the creation of Don Pedro's.

The subplot of *Much Ado about Nothing* may have the further effect of destabilizing the comic resolution, for if it has complicated and enriched our sense of the characters in the main plot, very much in spite of their best efforts to remain the kind of one-dimensional figures appropriate to a ro-

mance fiction, it makes it quite impossible to accept the excuses of Claudio
and Don Pedro when confronted with incontrovertible proof of Hero's innocence. "Yet sinn'd I not," says Claudio, "but in mistaking," and Don
Pedro is quick to second him: "By my soul, nor I" (V.i.274–75). But it is
simply too late to return from the complex depths the play has been plumb-
ing and have the kind of resolution appropriate to a comedy of innocent
mistakings.[17] The forgetting that is possible when injuries have been the result of impersonal forces seems unavailable here, for, as Northrop Frye has
observed, "To forget implies a break in the continuity of memory, a kind of
amnesia in which the previous action is put out of our reach. Normally, we
can forget in this way only when we wake up from a dream, when we pass
from one world into another, and we often have to think of the main action
of a comedy as 'the mistakes of a night,' as taking place in a dream or night-
mare world that the final scene suddenly removes us from and thereby
makes illusory."[18] In *Much Ado about Nothing* Shakespeare simply provides
us with no basis for such special pleading concerning Claudio's and Don
Pedro's vehement treatment of Hero, and especially concerning their callous
response to the news of her death. Indeed, as we have seen, the subplot suggests some explanations of their behavior that are illuminating but hardly
mitigating, and it is that much more to their discredit when Benedick, at
last presented in the form of Hero's apparent perfidy with what he might
well take as confirmation of his own cynical view of women, rises above his
misogyny and at the behest of Beatrice undertakes the defense of the lady's
reputation.

There are, of course, impersonal forces at work in *Much Ado about Nothing* moving to exculpate Hero and bring about a happy ending, however
qualified and tentative. These forces have no bearing on the inner life of
Claudio and Don Pedro, who remain in our eyes, with their lame excuses
about sinning only in mistaking, largely unreconstructed. Their inclusion in
the final harmony seems best described in a phrase of Dogberry's: they are
"condemn'd into everlasting redemption" (IV.ii.56–57). But to mention
Dogberry is to be reminded that impersonal forces do have effective, if not
exactly capable, agents, not only in the constable, but in the persons of
Verges and the members of the Watch, whose intuitive conviction about the
villainy of Borachio and energetic pursuit of the nonexistent Deformed finally lead to the discovery of Don John's plot and the exoneration of
Hero.[19] These unlikely ministers of providence (which more than lives up to
its reputation for moving in mysterious ways in this play) bring about a solution that has eluded all the better bred and putatively more incisive characters, and if they accomplish the feat without ever understanding the

nature of the crime (Dogberry calls it first "perjury," then "burglary" in IV.ii.42,50), their efforts nevertheless create the stir that finally leads to the truth. "What your wisdoms could not discover, these shallow fools have brought to light" (V.i.232–34), Borachio points out to the assembled men, rather to the detriment of their reputations for mature shrewdness. If Dogberry is to be writ down an ass, he must in all fairness be joined by a number of others who pride themselves on being in charge.

What Shakespeare has evidently given us in this unforgettable constable is an endlessly amusing portrait of a man with an unshakable conviction of his personal sovereignty, one who can suffer the most extraordinary reverses and misfirings of intention without appearing to notice. In short, he has given us a triumphant parody of the gentlemen characters for whom the distinction between themselves and Dogberry is as much a matter of settled conviction as Dogberry's own sense of his personal authority.[20] And perhaps with Dogberry, as with the gentlemen, his bland sense of being in control of the situation is ultimately shadowed by the nagging sense that he really is not:

> I am a wise fellow, and which is more, an officer,
> and which is more, a householder, and which is more,
> as pretty a piece of flesh as any is in Messina,
> and one that knows the law, go to, and a rich fellow
> enough, go to, and a fellow that hath had losses,
> and one that hath two gowns, and everything handsome
> about him. Bring him away. O that I had been
> writ down an ass!
>
> (IV.ii.80–87)

We never discover the nature of those "losses," incidentally tucked in between Dogberry's financial disclosures and his two gowns, but evidently his authority has not been sufficient to forestall them. One suspects that in those losses, whatever they may have been, we have the equivalent of the women the gentlemen characters cannot control but can only trust, the unacknowledged soft spot in the sovereignty they otherwise regard as absolute.

Language is, of course, the arena of Dogberry's most spectacular blunders, in all of which, not recognizing them as blunders, he finds abundant cogency. And, indeed, as in the case of "opinion'd" and "condemn'd into everlasting redemption," there is often in Dogberry's malapropisms a kind of weird propriety and pointedness not unlike the barbs of wit that Beatrice and Benedick aim at one another. A staple of their wit is the technique of willful mistaking, as when Beatrice affects to hear "And a good soldier too, lady" as "And a good soldier to a lady," and asks archly, "But what is he to a lord?" (I.i.53–55). Dogberry's misspeakings are very evidently inadvertent, while those of Beatrice and Benedick are just as evidently under the speaker's control, but it would be dangerous to conclude, as Benedick seems to do, that because he is a master of the intentional mistake, he is therefore proof against genuine mistaking. His constant misreading of his own feelings is a case in point, and this clear-eyed cynic, who congratulates himself on his shrewdness in keeping out of harm's way, is nevertheless radically deficient in self-knowledge, including the knowledge of his own vulnerability. But we should by this time be fully prepared for the characteristic Shakespearean effect of the master mastered, of "the enginer," in Hamlet's words, "Hoist with his own petar" (*Hamlet,* III.iv.206–7).

In fact, not one of the many schemes, plots, and practices that fill *Much Ado about Nothing* entirely succeeds in compassing its end, despite the boundless self-congratulation of the schemers, from Don Pedro's proxy wooing of Hero, which succeeds only after a number of misfires, to the Friar's plan to counterfeit Hero's death and thus fill Claudio with remorse and kind thoughts. That the latter scheme achieves nothing like its intended effect is one of the most disturbing things we know about Claudio, but it is also typical of the best-laid plans in this dramatic world. The men, at least, of *Much Ado about Nothing* are obsessive fashioners and contrivers, going about to encompass experience and make it conform to their wishes. But the play focuses the unstable relation between the plotter and his plot by playing on the word "fashion." Fashioning is, on the one hand, what the independent human artificer does, as when Don Pedro says of bringing Beatrice and Benedick together, "I doubt not but to fashion it" (II.i.368–69). But fashion in the sense of the current mode in dress and manners is also a fashioner in its turn, a transpersonal force, which, as Borachio knows, "giddily . . . turns about all the hot-bloods between fourteen and five-and-thirty, sometimes fashioning them like Pharaoh's soldiers in the reechy painting, sometime like god Bel's priests in the old church-window, sometime like the shaven Hercules in the smirch'd worm-eaten tapestry" (III.iii.131–37). That the fashioner is in his turn fashioned is a repeated irony in this play.

The inspired clowns of Shakespeare's two supreme romantic comedies, Touchstone in *As You Like It* and Feste in *Twelfth Night,* seem in possession of a truth toward which Shakespeare was tending during all his writing of comedy for the stage: wit is not allied with power and control but, as its etymological ancestry suggests, with wisdom. And the finest wit is only in part the product of studied artifice, for it has an aleatory component as well, and involves a willingness to surrender the self to what we would now call the work of the unconscious. Feste knows that wit is not something he can reliably deploy at need, for it must be wooed, invoked, prayed to: "Wit, and't be thy will, put me into good fooling! Those wits that think they have thee do very oft prove fools; and I that am sure I lack thee, may pass for a wise man" (*Twelfth Night,* I.v.32–35). Feste, although miles beyond Dogberry in point of self-awareness and sophistication, would none the less understand how it can happen that the constable's worst blunders sometimes have an inspired pertinence.

It is far from certain that the people of *Much Ado about Nothing* really learn the kind of lesson Feste has to teach and come to see the necessity for humble surrender. As many students of this play have pointed out, the bastard Don John makes an uncomfortably convenient focus for blame, a form of scapegoat familiar enough at the conclusion of Shakespeare's comedies.[21] As long as Don John can be designated, to use Ursula's words, as "the author of all" (V.ii.98–99), then castigation of the bastard is likely to replace humble introspection and the taking of personal stock. But Shakespeare himself seems to have taken the point onward through *As You Like It, Twelfth Night,* and beyond, for the confounding of those who would control and dictate is an important part of the late dark comedies, the so-called problem plays, as well. And it continues to be central through his very last play, no longer regarded as a real comedy but rather as a romance. In *The Tempest* Prospero at last voluntarily divests himself of his magical powers, not without regret and a nostalgic look backward at the astounding feats those powers have enabled him to perform. "But this rough magic / I here abjure" (V.i.50–51), he declares, and in so declaring reminds us that to the very end Shakespeare presents us with the paradox of a supreme artist who is profoundly skeptical about art itself.

## Chapter Six

# *As You Like It:* Textualized Nature and the Nature of the Text

*As You Like It* is with *Twelfth Night* one of the two great romantic comedies from Shakespeare's middle period. Its date is generally reckoned as 1599, making it roughly contemporary with *Julius Caesar* and *Henry V* and placing it on the threshold of the period of the mature tragedies, beginning with *Hamlet* (1600–1601). It has much in common with the later *Twelfth Night,* including the motif of cross-dressing, where a young woman in one or another kind of exile assumes a male identity (which on the stage is simply effected by adopting male costume) on the pretext of making herself secure in a world hostile to unprotected maidens. But the shift in sexual identity actually has implications that reach far beyond such literal motives, for in both *As You Like It* and *Twelfth Night* the heroine disguised as a young man uses her disguise and the roles it implies as a means of discovery, a way of testing the self and the others who pursue it. Disguise becomes the central instrument in a process of romantic comedy that moves, in C. L. Barber's phrase, "through release to clarification."[1]

But we should approach Barber's phrase with some care and diffidence, for what is implied by it is not some absolute release from constraint, an untrammeled saturnalian effusion of feeling and instinct, but a highly structured experience in which characters come to examine attitudes and postures, rejecting those that are found to be disharmonious with human nature and embracing, often in modified form, those that are found to be harmonious. This involves in *As You Like It* a playing out of various conventional roles, particularly those associated with the wooing of romantic love, a testing of various postures, some derived from purely literary conventions, that commit the posturer to one or another kind of asocial and self-involved behavior and impede rather than further the harmonious society at which the action of romantic comedy aims.

Once again, as with *A Midsummer Night's Dream,* I believe that it is a fundamental mistake to divide the play into two separate and distinct realms, the one (the court or the city) associated with the strictest constraint and the arbitrary rule of law, the other (a forest or some other form of "green world") with release and abandon, a kind of absolute freedom pure and simple. Such a division simply elides the fact that behavior in the forest is just as rule-bound and dictated as behavior in the court, though in the latter area dictation may be understood as impinging on the individual from the outside, while in the former it is understood as something interior to him, a matter of internalized codes and patterns.[2] But whether the individual is imposed upon by another or imposes on himself, we are justified in speaking of a form of tyranny, and the resolution finally achieved will always take shape as a compromise between individual desire and the transpersonal structures and sanctions that any human collective invokes (and must invoke) in order to achieve a measure of coherence and stability. If the title of the play we are currently considering, *As You Like It,* seems at first an unqualified invitation to self-indulgence, the offering of an opportunity for the uncontrolled release of personal desire, Shakespeare will remind us that what we like (and as we like it) is not always and only occasions for unhindered self-expression, but the rewards of achieving the fully social. Concerted and reciprocal action also has its gratifications.

But compromises are always, perhaps, inherently unstable, even when they have acquired the look of enduring solutions and static permanence. While it is not possible to dispense with the idea of compromise entirely, we should bear in mind that the play presents the relationships between various oppositions and antimonies as dialectical, that its apparently opposable categories are not simply placed over and against one another for purposes of mutual, if chilly, contemplation, but actually inhere in one another, with each member of such a relationship deriving its ground and means for being from its opposite number. Nowhere is this dialectical situation clearer than in what may seem to be the central opposition of the play as a whole, the great and apparently watertight categories of culture on the one hand and nature on the other. A little consideration will show that the play makes it remarkably difficult to sort out its various elements unequivocally according to this distinction. If, for instance, Orlando's infatuated habit of inscribing his love poems on the bark of trees seems an impossible (and very funny) attempt to textualize nature, designed to make it speak with a human voice (and we will see that everyone tries to do this in some manner and to some degree), we should not necessarily conclude therefore that there is nothing natural about the state of being in love, although we may continue to puzzle a good deal about how such a state might become manifest (short of sexual violence) without recourse to language, a recourse that always and inevitably entails the reintroduction of cultural categories.

Any discussion of the relationship between culture and nature in *As You Like It* will inevitably bring with it a consideration of Shakespeare's source for the play as well as the larger matter of the genre of pastoral poetry and the vogue for it in the fashionable literary circles of Shakespeare's day. Shakespeare's immediate source, Thomas Lodge's prose romance *Rosalynde; or, Euphues Golden Legacy* (1590), furnishes a charming example of the pastoral convention uncritically applied, and thus it has the advantage of rendering that convention in particularly pure form. Pastoral as Shakespeare knew it and exploited it for his own ends is always poetry (or very artful prose) about and, in theory, by shepherds, although it is necessary to qualify the concept of "shepherd" by noting that pastoral deals in shepherds of a remarkably rarefied and artful kind, romantically inclined, highly poetic beings whose actual labors in breeding, herding, protecting, and shearing sheep are attenuated to the point where they tend to disappear altogether. That raising sheep and marketing their wool considered as actual historical and economic activities involves a great deal of sweaty labor and privation is a brute fact that seldom if ever ruffles the surface of a pastoral poem. What the pastoral poet aims at is not the representation of economic relations and their attendant hardships, but the depiction of a series of refined postures and attitudes, the notion of communal life lived not merely in poetry, but, in fact, *as* poetry. It had always been thus in Shakespeare's time, stretching back to what is usually considered the ancient foundation of the genre with the Greek eclogues of the poet Theocritus in the third century B.C. Pastoral is, like comedy itself (and with which it is frequently allied), of the Western literary genres one of the most tenacious of its structures, themes, and procedures.

What should be clear is that pastoral poetry properly speaking is never the record of rural life produced by those who actually live it, but an idealized fantasy of rural life created by those who are excluded from it, the product of courtiers and aristocrats (or those who identify with them) aimed at the delectation of other courtiers and aristocrats, and, as such, a representation based on the wishful notion that life in nature is somehow simpler, purer, and more innocent than life in developed societies.[3] Bearing the aristocratic basis of pastoral poetry's vision of the country in mind, we should not be surprised to find that vision peopled by shepherds whose manners and speech are on the whole indistinguishable from those of courtiers (in Lodge's *Rosalynde,* for example, shepherds and courtiers alike speak the same mannered, "euphuistic" prose that Lodge imitated from the works of John Lyly),[4] as well as by a great many "shepherds" who are in fact courtiers masquerading as shepherds in order to escape the repressive rigors of life at court. The refugees always find it remarkably easy to adapt to their new home, largely because their new home is simply a model of their old home purged of the deviance and corruption that have driven them from their old home in the first place. The pastoral vision tries to straddle two worlds and combine both the benefits of innocent purity and the advantages of elitist status—a utopian attempt to have it both ways that we shall find Shakespeare's clown Touchstone poking considerable fun at.[5]

Pastoral poetry thus presents us with a radically thinned-out version of experience, where the possibilities of behavior and the opportunities for utterance are strictly limited to a narrow repertoire. Human converse in particular (and pastoral is a pervasively dialogic mode) is centered in but few topics (love, death, the advantages of mean estate), and all speech tends to become assimilated to one or another of the minor literary genres (complaint, elegy, encomium, love song). It is this last assimilation that explains why the pastoral scene so frequently includes the actual production of poetry, often in the form of a singing contest, the so-called amoebaean dialogue. In a world so self-consciously limited, where labor is reduced to a minimum and kept on the sidelines,[6] it is not difficult to see why all utterance verges on the recital of set pieces, and human action appears as a kind of attitudinizing engaged in for its own sake rather than directed toward exterior goals and purposes.

Lodge's *Rosalynde,* as indicated above, provides a relatively pure example of the pastoral genre, a "straight" rendition of its rules and procedures. Nothing is allowed to question the genre from within the fiction, no one points to what has been so carefully excluded, and the convention is simply played out according to the rules until the conventional happy ending in marriage is achieved. Such impatience as a reader may feel in contemplating so myopic a world cannot be counted as part of Lodge's meaning: it can only be assimilated as a failure of response, or as a failure of the text continuously to engage the reader's interest—in any case, as something adventitious to the story and the business it purports to be up to. The discerning reader who passes directly from Lodge's romance to Shakespeare's play is likely to notice that one thing distinguishing *As You Like It* from *Rosalynde* is that objections we might be expected to bring to the play have already been internalized in its dramatic fiction. We are relieved of the need to express impatience, simply because a number of characters on stage are rather eloquently expressing it for us, anticipating, as it were, our restlessness. If the pastoral convention is "framed" in Lodge's work simply by the boundaries of the work itself, the situation in Shakespeare's play is a good deal more complicated and interesting, for conventional action is always being framed and reframed within the fiction as the point of view shifts among attitudes bearing various degrees of assent.[7] Since Shakespeare otherwise hewed rather closely to the general outline and order of events in *Rosalynde,* it is surely significant that two of his characters, the comic Touchstone and the melancholy Jaques, have no precedent whatever in the source, for they are among Shakespeare's primary means for problematizing and placing at a distance the very convention by which *As You Like It* is otherwise structured.

But Shakespeare's resources for framing a given action and invoking attitudes out of reach of its conventional scope extend considerably beyond the deployment of detached characters who stand apart from various sequences and call them in question. The meeting of Rosalind, Celia, and Touchstone with Silvius and Corin as the former group enters Arden in II.iv provides a good example of the way Shakespeare has fused and juxtaposed a number of different kinds of fiction in *As You Like It,* any of which tends to provide a running comment on the others. Indeed, one of the chief sources of comedy in this play is the character who speaks from a limited generic and literary frame (well defined for us because it is surrounded by other frames), but speaks as if his current frame were the only one possible. Such is the case in II.iv when Silvius peremptorily denies that Corin has ever been in love:

> If thou rememb'rest not the slightest folly
> That ever love did make thee run into,
> Thou hast not lov'd;
> Or if thou hast not sat as I do now,
> Wearing thy hearer in thy mistress' praise,
> Thou hast not lov'd;
> Or if thou hast not broke from company
> Abruptly, as my passion now makes me,
> Thou hast not lov'd.
> O Phebe, Phebe, Phebe!                    *Exit.*
> (34–43)

Silvius's and Phebe's classicizing names are a dead giveaway of their status as conventional pastoral shepherds, the kind Shakespeare's audience would have been familiar with from countless examples of the pure genre. Silvius is simply the enamored swain, spurned by his cruel mistress, and he describes the kind of extravagant behavior conventionally assigned to the smitten but unrequited. The joke is, of course, that this impeccably pastoral shepherd, who seems to have stepped straight out of a romance, addresses himself to a character who might pass for a real shepherd. At least Corin seems to engage in the actual labor of tending sheep, has an absentee master who is "of churlish disposition" (80), and works on land that is a real economic entity and is up for sale (83–84). The sense of two mutually exclusive frames failing to communicate with one another is an early instance of the kind of impasse Shakespeare will exploit throughout the forest sequence.[8]

But Silvius's short aria here has further interest, because it provides an example of the kind of downright prescriptiveness we will meet in every corner of the Forest of Arden. He is one of a series of characters in *As You Like It* who attempt, with various degrees of rigor and intransigence, to impose their own views and constructs on others, to claim what is, after all, a thoroughly subjective vision of the world as a standard and a norm. Denying another's assertion that he has been in love is something like denying his assertion that he is angry—"No, you're not" is an unaccountable and absurd rejoinder in such a situation. Silvius's prescriptiveness about the marks of the lover is undoubtedly comic: the true lover is, after all, according to Silvius's formula, he who behaves ridiculously, manages to bore the life out of his interlocutor, and then breaks off the conversation rudely. The formula simply reduces what might otherwise be the true symptoms of love to its mere signs, signs that are in principle subject to appropriation and imitation by anyone, whether true lover or no. The attempt to "naturalize" a point of view in this way finds its most extreme expression in the figures of the tyrannical Frederick and Oliver in the world of the court, but it is again a measure of the continuity of the worlds of court and forest—and not of the differences between them—that we find a related will to impose throughout the sequence in the forest. If tyranny transposed to the forest seems more benign than the threatening and melodramatic cruelty of Frederick and Oliver, we can nevertheless recognize in the pastoral community something like the same competitiveness and will to power that is at the root of civilized corruption.

Still, certain crucial differences are easy to specify. What makes the forest's version of tyranny so much less threatening than the version we encounter at court is in one sense the restored possibility for playfulness, the opportunities for exploratory role-playing that the country setting offers. In the corrupt court of Duke Frederick true playfulness has either disappeared or become brutalized to the point where it no longer qualifies as playfulness. So much is at stake, for instance, in the lethal wrestling match that

Frederick has arranged (and that Oliver tries to use as a means of killing Orlando) that it can no longer be called a game, although we may recognize in it an emblem of the vicious brutality subtending the social organization. Definition of the self in this situation is not so much a matter of self-definition as it is a matter of the whim of the ruler, or the system of affiliations into which the self is born and over which it exercises no control. In either case the means of creating identity are for the individual always elsewhere, always beyond the reach of his will. On hearing, for instance, that Orlando is the youngest son of Sir Rowland de Boys, Frederick responds in characteristically arbitrary fashion:

> I would thou hadst been son to some man else:
> The world esteem'd thy father honorable,
> But I did find him still mine enemy.
> Thou shouldst have better pleas'd me with this deed
> Hadst thou descended from another house.
>
> (I.ii.224–28)

These lines deny Orlando the very possibility of self-definition, for they lodge his value (or from Frederick's point of view, the lack of it) entirely in Orlando's ancestry and not at all in his "deed," the besting of Charles in the wrestling match.

The lines also reveal something about Frederick's insanely antisocial attitude, for they allow us to define it as the insistent refusal of social consensus, in this case the good opinion that the world at large has accorded Orlando's father. Without denying that there is something finally arbitrary about the conferral of value on the individual by consensus (the means of defining the self in this case are still from the point of view of the individual elsewhere—we never escape the tyranny of the other in this sense), it is still possible to say that Frederick's brand of arbitrariness forecloses certain possibilities for forming new consensuses on the one hand, and for checking and modifying those already formed on the other. Ideally, a social consensus is built up at least in part by collective response to the initiatives of the individual. If such response is dictated in its turn by a prior consensus about what constitutes value, this is not to deny that both are subject in a flexible and open organization to various kinds of testing and modification. But when the process of consensus is replaced by the tyrant's whim—perhaps because of his buried fear of the collective tyranny of consensus formation—clearly all possibility of collective testing and adjustment is put out of question.

We are now in a better position to see what kinds of possibilities, suppressed by the tyranny of Frederick's court, are restored in the flight to the Forest of Arden. Once again, it is not that the will to tyrannize and dictate, the itch to control situations absolutely, is somehow abolished by the forest setting in favor of an unproblematic freedom, but that the new setting seems to offer the renewed possibility of dialogue, of reciprocity and exchange in human intercourse. It may strike us in this new context that the dialogic in human affairs is precisely what Duke Frederick's arbitrary sway has foreclosed. When Rosalind has been branded a traitor, for instance, she attempts to initiate an exchange with the duke:

> *Ros.* Yet your mistrust cannot make me a traitor.
> Tell me whereon the likelihood depends.
> *Duke F.* Thou art thy father's daughter, there's
>      enough.
>
> (I.iii.56–58)

Rosalind is in one sense wrong here—where only one voice counts, its mistrust can, indeed, "make" her a traitor, for the prior dialogue between individual initiative and social consensus has been overridden by the duke's refusal of the dialogic in all its forms and at all levels. The tyrant comes to dictate not only behavior, but meaning itself, for he determines by fiat the criteria in virtue of which value-bearing terms like "traitor" will be applied.

Meaning in the forest is once again very much liberated from this tyranny of a single corrupt will, and, although there is, as I have noted, an abundance of attempts to reappropriate it, none is quite successful, because each encounters a restraining and qualifying force either in the form of another person attempting to appropriate meaning for himself, or a wit like Touchstone or Rosalind, who calls all meanings into question by way of testing the validity of what we normally take for granted.[9] Jaques is perhaps the most extreme example the forest offers of one who tries to override dialogue and be the only voice heard, and again, if his morose insistence on his own point of view seems relatively unthreatening and can be contained (though at times uneasily) within the prevailing comic mood, it is because he is continually forced into exchanges with others in the forest. Indeed, there is something comically paradoxical in Jaques's misanthropy, for what the misanthrope, the scorner of mankind in general, needs above all is precisely mankind in the form of an audience. If you are a misanthrope, you badly need somebody to listen to your diatribe.[10]

So powerful is the drive to override dialogue in Jaques that we may be surprised to find it even in places where it seems unlikely to surface. His triumphant discovery of Touchstone and the role of the professional fool, for instance, which he recounts in a long exchange with Duke Senior in the second act, may lead us to expect something other than an altruistic motive in his ambition to become a fool and satirist:

> I must have liberty
> Withal, as large a charter as the wind,
> To blow on whom I please, for so fools have;
> And they that are most galled with my folly,
> They most must laugh. And why, sir, must they so?
> The why is plain as way to parish church:
> He that a fool doth very wisely hit
> Doth very foolishly, although he smart,
> Not to seem senseless of the bob; if not,
> The wise man's folly is anatomiz'd
> Even by the squand'ring glances of the fool.
> (II.vii.47–57)

Jaques's rationale is drawn from a traditional defense of satire, where it is claimed, among other things, that the satirist is a reformer interested in attacking vices and not individuals, and that individuals guilty of those vices are not held up to public scorn, because they need not protest the satirist's allegations, but may quietly set about reforming themselves in private.[11] But we may well suspect that what really attracts Jaques to the grandiose project of cleansing "the foul body of th' infected world" (60) is precisely the immunity from rejoinder that the office of satirist seems to confer. To answer him is to convict yourself of vice or social deviation, and thus the satirist is assured that his voice will be the only one heard. Given the myopic one-sidedness of Jaques's attitude, it is not surprising that it never occurs to him in telling of his meeting with the moralizing Touchstone ("And so from hour to hour, we ripe and ripe, / And then from hour to hour, we rot and rot" [26–27]) that Touchstone has not been offering a seriously intended philosophical observation about the world but a wonderfully apt parody of Jaques himself.

This attempt to expand a limited and personal frame to include all others and silence all voices but one's own is, of course, here reframed in its turn by the very fact that Jaques must explain his satirical project in a dialogue and expose it to the objections of other points of view. Thus to

Jaques's insistence that he would accomplish nothing "but good" (63), Duke Senior rejoins:

> Most mischievous foul sin, in chiding sin:
> For thou thyself hast been a libertine,
> As sensual as the brutish sting itself,
> And all th' embossed sores, and headed evils,
> That thou with license of free foot has caught,
> Wouldst thou disgorge into the general world.
>                                               (64–69)

These lines themselves are drawn from the traditional debate about satire and the satirist, and they express the recurrent suspicion that the satirist, whatever he may claim in the way of disinterested public spiritedness, is really engaged in a personal vendetta or simply giving vent to an inherently bilious temperament. This is not to say that this long exchange settles the question of the status of satire or the nature of the satirist's motives: what is important for our view of *As You Like It* in general is that it ventilates Jaques's extreme subjectivist position and reinserts it into a dialogic situation.

Such ventilation lies at the very heart of the play, for it is central to Rosalind's complex impersonation, first of Ganymede, then further of "Rosalind," the stand-in for the lady in the practice wooing in which both she and Orlando engage. This central situation is of the greatest interest, because it tends to pick up and parodically refract so many of the thematic and rhetorical strains at large in the play as a whole. What is most striking about Rosalind and her double impersonation is simply the range of postures she strikes without allowing any one to take over the situation or herself.[12] Unlike Orlando, or Jaques, or the rejected Silvius, all of whom play ultimately monotonous roles that they are not quite aware of as roles, Rosalind's far more self-conscious playfulness allows her to try out various postures and attitudes, to entertain ideas (in the broadest sense) without having to invite them in as permanent guests.

Rosalind thus enjoys a certain freedom and perspective denied to those who allow themselves to be entirely determined by the roles they have chosen. Indeed, it is precisely the anterior moment of choice that has been forgotten in such instances, a forgetting that conveniently allows a character to promote a mere role, one possibility among others, to the status of his inevitable, single, unified "nature," a promotion that represents a conflation of what he says and does with what he is. In the case of the lover, this process is likely to include the claim to uniqueness, which, as we saw in *A Midsummer Night's Dream,* has the paradoxical effect of showing the utter conventionality of the lover's behavior. Silvius says of his passion, "I think did never man love so" (II.iv.29), and Orlando's verse is an extended and hyperbolic claim for Rosalind as a nonpareil.

Thus Rosalind playing Ganymede playing "Rosalind" (and this laminated impersonation already shows that she is not confined by a single role) manages to mock most of the elements that Orlando's seriously undertaken attempt to be the moonstruck lover entails. The lover's claim to punctilious and intransigent devotion, for instance, his putatively religious dedication to the beloved, becomes in Rosalind's parody an insistence on punctuality:

> By my troth, and in good earnest, and so
> God mend me, and by all the pretty oaths that
> are not dangerous, if you break one jot of your
> promise, or come one minute behind your hour, I
> will think you the most pathetical break-promise,
> and the most hollow lover, and the most unworthy
> of her you call Rosalind, that may be chosen out
> of the gross band of the unfaithful; therefore
> beware my censure, and keep your promise.
> (IV.i.188–96)

This is more complicated than it may first appear, for while insisting on keeping promises to the letter, Rosalind manages to cast a skeptical glance at the whole institution of lovers' promises, the folly of binding the self so minutely, the shortsightedness of not realizing that contingency may intervene to modify any promise, as indeed it does in the next scene but one, when Orlando's wound prevents him from keeping his appointment. And the multiple oaths ("By my troth, and in good earnest, and so God mend me") tend to call attention to the act of swearing rather than to what is sworn, leaving us with the suspicion that lovers' promises are a mere form of words and, as such, more a rhetorical performance than a real vow.

Indeed, it is possible to see something rather melancholy in the ventilation of the conventional lover's posture that Rosalind undertakes in IV.i., as she counters Orlando's hopelessly idealized version of lover and beloved with a portrait rather less flattering. Her very witty account of men and women insists on the all-too-real possibilities of foibles, perversities, breaches of faith, and further on the flat certainties of human mutability, the passage of time, death:

> Say "a day," without the "ever." No, no,
> Orlando, men are April when they woo, December
> when they wed; maids are May when they are maids,
> but the sky changes when they are wives.
> (IV.i.146–49)

These are things that Orlando's framing of the relationship between lover and beloved has simply left out of account, much in the way the pastoral frame excludes labor and sometimes even sheep. But they are indubitably possibilities and exigencies that must be reckoned with, if any relationship is to have value and endure.

And yet it would be in its way just as sentimental as Orlando's romantic drooling to insist that the hardheaded and even cynical vision of men and women that Rosalind offers in response is somehow the true view replacing a false one, in some sense "reality" unalloyed. It is always a mistake simply to identify the real in literature with the unpleasant and gritty, an identification that a series of hard-boiled, if rather undistinguished, novels in our own time has encouraged us to make.[13] One thing that militates against taking Rosalind's merry and cynical suggestions as her seriously offered version of reality is that the suggestions are not really offered by Rosalind but by "Rosalind," an improvised character of the game in which she and Orlando are engaged. In placing her own name in quotation marks Rosalind further places all that she utters as "Rosalind" in quotation marks, with the effect of rendering all assertion provisional, the enunciation of a possibility, rather than the pronouncement of a certainty. With the pretense of being as whimsically tyrannical as any character in the play, Rosalind actually contrives to dispel tyranny. And in liberating Orlando from the tyranny of the role he is uncritically playing, she also liberates his (and our) ability to extract whatever truths conventional love rhetoric really does contain.

We may also note that she accomplishes something like the same for herself. One of the dangers of Orlando's unexamined posturing is that it is always in danger of becoming a vehicle for his own narcissism. As Rosalind observes of Orlando on the occasion of their first meeting in the forest, "You are rather point-device in your accoustrements, as loving yourself, than seeming the lover of any other" (III.ii.382–84). One who goes about hanging sonnets on bushes and carving love poems on trees, after all, opens himself to the suspicion that what he is really inviting is not admiration for the lady who is the subject of those poems, not even, perhaps, admiration for the poems themselves, but precisely admiration for the poet.[14] There is always something unmistakably self-indulgent about Orlando as moonstruck

lover. But Rosalind runs the related risk of simply seconding Orlando's posture, and this for the very good reason that, however absurd it is to be the
subject of poems pinned up all over the forest, it is also very flattering. It
takes a great deal of ironic distance to resist the temptation of vanity, and in
placing herself in quotation marks, rendering herself as open possibility
rather than the fixed and radically reduced personality that is the appropriate object of idolatrous adoration, Rosalind not only cures Orlando of love
poetry, she controls whatever inclinations she has to think of herself as the
appropriate subject of such poetry. What makes her scolding of Silvius and
Phebe somewhat less harsh than it seems is our recognition that Rosalind is
at the same time scolding herself indirectly:

> 'Tis not her glass, but you that flatters her,
> And out of you she sees herself more proper
> Than any of her lineaments can show her.
> But, mistress, know yourself, down on your knees,
> And thank heaven, fasting, for a good man's love;
> For I must tell you friendly in your ear,
> Sell when you can, you are not for all markets.
> (III.v.54–60)

This ability to talk about the self in the process of talking to and about others is altogether characteristic of the way Rosalind's complex impersonation
disperses the specious conviction of the unity of the self and opens it up to
possibility, experimentation, and finally growth.

The view of the individual and his capabilities implicit in Rosalind's
games in the forest could not be further, when we come to think of it, from
the countervailing view implied by what is perhaps the best-known and frequently quoted passage in *As You Like It,* Jaques's speech on "The Seven
Ages of Man." But perhaps no single Shakespearean set piece better shows
the folly of quoting lines out of context and then identifying them as
Shakespeare's wisdom or some sort of general truth about our human condition. Context makes it clear that the speech is, in fact, one more expression
of Jaques's extreme subjectivity, and its declamatory style of delivery one
more example of his fondness for having the floor to himself. "All the
world's a stage," Jaques begins (as all the world knows),

> And all the men and women merely players;
> They have their exits and their entrances,

And one man in his time plays many parts,
His acts being seven ages.

(II.vii.140–43)

There follows the familiar (and rather depressing) progression from mewling and puking infant through whining schoolboy, sighing lover, swearing soldier, obese justice, shrunken elder, until we come full circle to second childishness, "Sans teeth, sans eyes, sans taste, sans everything" (166). What may strike us, especially if we come at the speech by way of Rosalind's wooing game, is that for Jaques a role is not a way of introducing new directions and opening up potentials, but a course imposed on the individual from the outside, a tyrannically deterministic scenario, in which we are all simply programmed to follow the dreary round from childhood to second childishness.

We may also suspect that with his detached bearing and faintly contemptuous tone Jaques means to imply his own exemption from the unenviable fate he ascribes to the rest of us—a not uncommon effect in those who would give us the true view or the big picture. But it is surely striking that it is Jaques himself who is determined, if not by the circular course described in his speech, then at least by the immediate context. It is seldom noticed that "The Seven Ages of Man" speech is in one sense simply a rhetorical expansion of Touchstone's "And so from hour to hour, we ripe and ripe, / And then from hour to hour, we rot and rot" (II.vii.26– 27). "And thereby hangs a tale" (28), Touchstone has said rather cryptically of his mock-melancholy observation, and we have every reason to believe that in his subsequent speech Jaques is simply attempting to supply the tale that Touchstone has rather wisely left hanging. Jaques's authority and license to give us the true view thus derive from a very witty clown, who, so far from offering the truth about life, has been doing, as we have seen, a mocking imitation of Jaques himself, who has, quite simply, failed to grasp the frame of his encounter with Touchstone.

In spite of Jaques's repeated attempts to find parallels between himself and Touchstone, to claim, in fact, Touchstone's office of fool and jester, it is clear that Rosalind is the one character in the play who has a true affinity with the professional fool.[15] The difference, of course, is obvious and important: Rosalind's foolery is a temporary measure aimed at moving Orlando off the dead center of romantic lover. Once this has been accomplished, she exchanges her ironic detachment for emotional investment in the world once again, although it is a world substantially transformed by her own irony. We are far less likely to see Touchstone's marriage to Audrey as an emotional investment, and in any case it seems unlikely that he will ever abandon his detached relationship to those with whom he consorts, although we can be sure that he will continue to consort and not, like Jaques at the end, choose a life of solitude. The fool, for all his detachment and obliquity, is still an essentially social being, a member of the collective, although it may not always be easy to specify the nature of his participation.

But we should not allow this central difference between Rosalind and Touchstone to obscure the very real similarities. Both characters enjoy the kind of freedom that allows them to take up positions temporarily, to try out a variety of points of view without necessarily committing the self to any one, to test reality in order to discover if it is worthy of the name. The result, among other things, is that of all the characters in *As You Like It* Rosalind and Touchstone are the most difficult to contain within a continuous and stable frame, for they both shift stance with great speed and are even capable—often by means of an elaborate and punning wordplay—of occupying more than one position simultaneously. If this ability gives them a certain protected superiority to those with whom they consort, it also leaves them vulnerable to misinterpretation on the part of audience and characters alike. We have already seen how Jaques misinterprets his first meeting with Touchstone (as opposed to Corin and Audrey, who form no interpretations whatever, but are simply reduced to puzzled silence in his presence), and Celia will similarly misinterpret Rosalind after her long exchange with Orlando in IV.i:

> You have simply misus'd our sex in your love-
> prate. We must have your doublet and hose
> pluck'd over your head, and show the world what
> the bird hath done to her own nest.
>
> (201–4)

Celia has failed to grasp the tentative and playful character of Rosalind's misogynistic remarks; she has framed them as a straight statement of seriously held beliefs, much as Jaques has taken Touchstone's melancholy meditation as a sincerely offered philosophical statement about life.

This kind of misframing within the play should alert us against the possibility of doing the like, particularly with Touchstone's more whimsical and complicated exchanges. In his pleasant, if puzzling, little interlude with Corin at the beginning of the third act (and the forest sequence as a whole is really a succession of such conversational interludes—very little happens in the ordinary sense), we have already glanced at the fact that he begins by exploding the contradictory wishes in those who have fled to the forest and ultimately in the pastoral genre itself. "How like you this shepherd's life, Master Touchstone?" Corin inquires politely. Touchstone replies with an air of cogency:

> Truly, shepherd, in respect of itself, it is
> a good life; but in respect that it is a shepherd's
> life, it is naught. In respect that it is solitary,
> I like it very well; but in respect that it is
> private, it is a very vild life. Now in respect
> it is in the fields, it pleaseth me well; but in
> respect it is not in the court, it is tedious. As
> it is a spare life (look you) it fits my humor well;
> but as there is no more plenty in it, it goes much
> against my stomach.
>
> (III.ii.13–22)

Wishing the court natural and nature courtly is the kind of contradiction that subtends Orlando's absurd scrawling of poetry on trees: he wants to textualize the natural, to make it speak with a human voice, at the same time that he may imagine that his contrived and artificial verses will gain spontaneity by virtue of their inscription on trees—in short that the text will be naturalized. Something like the same contradiction informs Duke Senior's speech at the beginning of the forest sequence, though with nothing like the effect of Orlando's absurdly literal-minded tree writing, when he speaks of finding "tongues in trees, books in the running brooks" (II.i.16). Touchstone's complaint that the court has no fields and the fields have no court merely brings such contradictions to the surface and mocks all attempts at reconciling them.

Touchstone goes on to take what appears to be one of the most imperious stances in *As You Like It* in insisting to Corin that the court is the standard by which all else must be judged and that Corin himself is damned, because he has never been at court. We should, however, be wary of falling into Jaques's error and assuming that meaning and intention simply coincide in Touchstone's discourse. Rather than posit a pragmatic intention for his argument—persuading Corin of the error of his ways and the superiority of life at court, for instance—we may assume that he is simply trying out a point of view rather than espousing it, much in the way we have seen Rosalind as Ganymede as "Rosalind" take up an antifeminist position without for a minute becoming misogynistic. It is the ability to maintain an ironic aloofness from one's own assertions that the fool very much shares with the heroine.

In the present instance, the joke that results from this implicit disclaiming of what is said (and note that Touchstone implicitly disclaims not only the substance of what he says, but the imperious style he uses to lay claim to it) is that Corin ends up arguing like a courtier and Touchstone like a countryman. It is Corin who expresses the fastidiousness we normally associate with the refined and educated man, Touchstone who expresses the robust and earthy views we normally associate with the shepherd. The fool will have none of Corin's queasy delicacy about countrymen greeting one another by the courtly means of kissing hands, for if shepherds' hands are greasy, the courtiers' hands sweat, if shepherd's hands are rough, "Your lips will feel them the sooner," and if they are covered with tar, that is yet preferable to the courtier's hand perfumed with civet, for civet is "the very uncleanly flux of a cat" (III.ii.45–69).

There is something uncanny in this crisscrossing of apparently firm positions, for Touchstone has evidently succeeded in putting language at such a distance, at casting assertion so far adrift from its mooring in pragmatic intention, that it may begin to seem that any argument can in principle come to be invaded by its antithesis. When discourse is not so much to be understood as a production originating in the speaker but as a parodic citation of a point of view the speaker does not necessarily share, truculent imperiousness will be thoroughly undermined, and human rigidity will seem to dissolve in the destabilizing fact that all meaning is achieved by the exclusion of other meanings, and that a particularly emphatic assertion will always stir the suspicion that the emphasis is necessary not because what is emphasized is true, but precisely because it is not.[16] Protesting too much, as Gertrude observes of the player queen in *Hamlet* (III.ii.230), is the surest way to call your position in question. In abandoning himself to a point of view, Touchstone succeeds in subverting not only Corin's position but his own as well, and he may just dramatize the ultimate absurdity of taking up any position at all, at least with the unbending rigor of Oliver and Frederick, or the comic stubbornness of Jaques, or the formulaic inflexibility of Orlando and Silvius and Phebe.

In dismissing Corin's commonsense explanations of why shepherds do not greet one another in the courtly manner, Touchstone also provokes a central meditation on the nature of convention. Corin insists that polite conventions are based on concrete circumstances and that their presence or absence in a given situation is strictly motivated by material conditions. While this is a plausible position on the face of it, Touchstone's hyperbolic denials must make us wonder whether conventions are ever quite so simply explained. In showing that courtiers' hands are quite as distasteful as shepherds' when contemplated as objects of kissing, he manages to give the custom of hand kissing the specious look of a metaphysical imperative. The argument is further enabled by equating manners with morals, a sophistic move (but again, this is sophistry that knows itself as such) made possible by the semantic stretch of the word "manners" in Shakespeare's English: "If thou never saw'st good manners, then thy manners must be wicked, and wickedness is sin, and sin is damnation" (III.ii.41–43). Touchstone exploits the fact that "manners" may refer either to a code of etiquette or to behavior subject to praise or censure in the moral sense. In sliding from the first sense to the second, he speciously naturalizes courtly customs and suggests that Corin's failure to practice them imperils his immortal soul. Touchstone's argument is, of course, a virtuoso parody of all the many attempts in the play to naturalize a point of view, to claim for mere subjectivity one or another kind of metaphysical sanction.

The fool thus transfers the origin of conventions from the material sphere of Corin's argument to the metaphysical sphere. And yet the peremptory vehemence with which he puts the argument will inevitably insinuate the possibility of its antithesis—that conventions originate neither in material conditions nor in metaphysical imperatives, but are simply the result of a community's consensus about what constitutes "proper" behavior and are thus not motivated at all in the sense that one community's consensus may work just as well (or poorly) as another's. But it is not quite possible to come to rest even here, for Touchstone's hyperbolic moral argument puts us in mind that any community needs some code in which it is possible for one person to express deference to another, some set of procedures for yielding the floor, for expressing one's sense of the other's needs and sensibilities, or simply for maintaining reciprocity. The fool's extravagant insistence that behaving properly is the only way for the individual to escape damnation tends to banish such merely social considerations, and yet they return precisely in Corin's homely and "shallow" instances, which at bottom rest on a concern lest one offend others. The ultimate effect of the intransigent position the fool takes up is to collapse the very difference between court and country that he begins with.

"Much virtue in If," Touchstone remarks in the final scene of *As You Like It* (V.iv.103). There is some richness in the very simplicity of this remark. It refers immediately to a way of releasing oneself from the absurd punctilio of the dueling code that Touchstone has been expounding for Jaques, a code similar in interesting ways to the prescriptive scenario of "The Seven Ages of

Man" speech. But it refers beyond the immediate moment as well to the whole issue, of provisionality and tentativeness so central to the way Rosalind and Touchstone take up positions without espousing them, the way these characters free language of immediate pragmatic intent in order to pose the question "What if?" The range of answers forthcoming will be generated more by the position itself than by the subject temporarily occupying that position, encumbered as he is by all his desires and biases and special pleading. Placing the self in quotation marks and citing a point of view rather than committing the self to it are ways of eliminating the opportunities social converse otherwise offers for badgering and domineering.

The play thus moves from the tyrannical imperatives of Frederick's court to the playful subjunctives of the forest, and if the conclusion foreshadows a return, we have some assurance that it will be a return to a court where the impulse to tyrannize will be checked by a better understanding of the many forms tyranny can take. It is not that *As You Like It* holds out the sentimental hope that every kind of arbitrariness can simply be swept away. But if Jaques's refusal to join the celebration at the end, because, as he says, he is "for other than for dancing measures" (V.iv.193), seems a refusal of the kind of constraint social life inevitably entails, it is still significant that the revelers do not press him on the matter, for that would be to exercise the very tyranny the experience in the forest has otherwise succeeded in mitigating.

## Chapter Seven

# *Twelfth Night:* The Trick of Singularity

The forest games in *As You Like It* have the pretext of filling an enforced suspension in the lives of those who participate. They are a way of making the best of a bad situation, of filling the temporary pause in normal life forced upon the courtly participants by the tyrannizing of Frederick and Oliver. But no such enforced temporal hiatus underlies the aristocrats and their doings in *Twelfth Night,* and the posturing and impersonating seem typical of daily life in Illyria, not the extraordinary behavior appropriate to a temporal interlude. If the Forest of Arden is treated as a kind of retreat for the duration, a place from which to stage a return to society, Illyria is all the society *Twelfth Night* offers, and the comic milieu ends up absorbing those who have participated in it, natives and newcomers alike. We may see certain similarities in each case, particularly in those who persist in rejecting society at the conclusion, notably Jaques and Malvolio, but the character of Malvolio's final refusal is altogether different from Jaques's. It is not at all a decision to retreat further (there is no place further to retreat), nor is it really a decision so much as an impassioned determination to "be reveng'd on the whole pack" of comic revelers (V.i.378), not only those responsible for Malvolio's victimization, but those who have had nothing whatever to do with it. We can have no feeling that Malvolio, like Jaques, is exercising an option at the end of *Twelfth Night,* for he seems still passionately obsessed, and whether the attempt to "entreat him to a peace" (V.i.380) will succeed or fail is a question the play leaves very much undecided. What is clear is that there can be no simple parting of the ways in Illyria as there is in Arden, for the single way of Illyria fills the dramatic fiction to its edges. To exit from Illyria is to exit from the play itself.

This may help to explain why some critics have found the atmosphere of *Twelfth Night* somewhat stuffy and enervating, at least in comparison to the merry and energetic activity that pervades the Forest of Arden. In *As You Like It* narcissistic self-involvement seems generally and amusingly a fault of youth, something that can in principle be educated out of the aberrant individual. Even at the height of his romanticism Orlando can reply to Jaques's invitation to rail against the world, "I will chide no breather in the world but myself, against whom I know most faults" (III.ii.280–81). We cannot seriously worry about someone who preserves that kind of perspective on himself, even if he does seem otherwise rather silly and self-indulgent. In *Twelfth Night,* on the other hand, self-involvement seems endemic in the society of Illyria, a pervasive malaise, rather than an isolated, altogether amusing deviance.[1] The only characters substantially free of it, Viola and the detached Feste, are significantly outsiders, aliens by happenstance or election to the rather languid posturing of Orsino and Olivia, or the perpetually drunken antics of Sir Toby, or—in a very different mood and register—the brutally egotistic fantasies of Malvolio. Viola will go to work on the first two as Feste will go to work on the last, but her success is achieved only with a massive assist from what is variously called "Fate" or "Time," and his, which is effected wholly through human contrivance, is not really achieved at all. The plot to bring Malvolio some measure of self-awareness (if it really is that, and not just what many have seen as a cruel practical joke) is apparently an utter failure.

It is possible to glimpse something of the self-enclosed quality of *Twelfth Night* at the very outset in the juxtaposition of its first two scenes. The first is remarkable in the way it withholds exposition, fails to locate the action in time or space. The initial speaker is not named, and if we discover by the way some details about his beloved, including her name, our curiosity is scarcely piqued, precisely because the speaker seems so indifferent to the lady as a creature of flesh and blood. He is utterly unperturbed by the news that she has vowed to sequester herself for seven years, and we may be led to suspect that his is a love not in need of an object, because it has already found a sufficient one in himself. Whoever this strange man may be, with his high-strung rhetoric delivered in a void, he lives entirely in his own thoughts in an apparent attempt to consume the world and subdue it to fantasy:

> O spirit of love, how quick and fresh art thou,
> That notwithstanding thy capacity
> Receiveth as the sea, nought enters there,
> Of what validity and pitch so'er,
> But falls into abatement and low price
> Even in a minute. So full of shapes is fancy
> That it alone is high fantastical.
>
> (I.i.9–15)

It is an odd sort of love, it may strike us, that abolishes differences and deflates all value—including, it would seem, that of the lady herself.[2]

After such suffocating enclosure it is refreshing to find in the scene following a sensibility turned toward the world, actively probing its mysteries, a sensibility that, in spite of the good reasons it has for withdrawal and mourning, is still actively interested in the here and now. Viola's brisk and direct questions are met by the captain's equally direct answers: "What country, friends, is this? This is Illyria, lady" (I.ii.1–2); "Who governs here? A noble duke, in nature as in name. What is his name? Orsino" (24–27). Viola's active interrogation balances Orsino's passive indifference, just as her abrupt resolve to adopt male attire and serve the duke as a page balances his languid refusal to do anything whatever. If Viola's motivation for disguising herself is not yet clear (and it is, perhaps, never entirely clarified), such questions as we have are thrust aside in our relief that at least someone in this play has determination and resource. We, after all, cannot wait the seven years that Orsino seems willing to wait for the action to begin.

We discover in this second scene not only a contrast between Viola and Orsino, but a contrast (which is ultimately far more a parallel) between Viola and Olivia as well. Both women mourn a lost brother (although Sebastian will finally be restored to Viola), Olivia by retreating into obsessive memory and the sterile repetition of her sense of loss, Viola by taking characteristic action in memorializing her absent brother by internalizing his masculine nature, by becoming him in a provisional sense. This proves an inspired gesture not only because it serves "to season / A brother's dead love" (I.i.29–30) in a sense quite different from what the phrase means as originally applied to Olivia's obsessive mourning,[3] but also because it allows Viola to test, in the manner of her counterpart Rosalind, the limits of her own masculine component, to clarify the real differences between the sexes by experimenting with what they have in common.[4] "I can sing / And speak to him in many sorts of music" (I.ii.57–58), Viola observes in anticipation of her relationship to Orsino, and it is precisely her complex command of multiple registers and pitches, her ability to modulate in and out of the various styles and tones that are offered, often with rigid single-mindedness, by the other characters in the play that allows her to make discoveries about them as well as about herself. "How dost thou like this tune?" Orsino will ask the character he has come to think of as Cesario, and Viola will reply in a manner that improves on (by chastening) Orsino's own extravagant rhetoric, "It gives a very echo to the seat / Where Love is thron'd"

(II.iv.21–22). Orsino's response, "Thou dost speak masterly," is true in ways that he ,cannot yet imagine.

And yet this giving of the self to a disguise and thence to the variety of postures the disguise allows is fraught with certain risks about which the play as a whole, if not its heroine at the outset, is very clear. "Conceal me what I am," Viola asks the captain, "and be my aid / For such disguise as haply shall become / The form of my intent" (I.ii.53–55). She means, of course, that she seeks a disguise appropriate to her plan, one that will further it ("become" in the sense of "befit"). But she cannot quite avoid suggesting that the disguise may take her over, that it will become (in the sense of "change into") the form of her intent and, according to a logic of its own, commit her to unforeseen courses of action and embroil her in unanticipated entanglements. We need look no further than Olivia's precipitate infatuation with one she takes to be an attractive young man for an example of such difficulty. Disguise, like the very language Viola here uses to speak of it, has a way of committing the user to meanings and stances beyond the user's will, of inverting the relationship so that user becomes used, his intention canceled by the independent logic of the means he has chosen to effect it.[5] Means have their own meanings as well (they are never simply transparent to the intentions they are supposed to serve), and the indispensable means of language in particular always harbor the possibility of meaning in excess of the user's intent. Even the "masterly" speaker cannot limit the verb "become" to a single meaning.[6]

This opacity of means and mediation in *Twelfth Night* makes Viola's role problematic in a way that Rosalind's in *As You Like It* is not. If Rosalind as Ganymede infatuates Phebe, the resulting tangle is still relatively free of conflict, because Phebe's infatuation in no way compromises Rosalind's relation to Orlando. But Viola's disguise commits her to contradictory loyalties. She is bound as Orsino's servant to perform his bidding as surrogate wooer of Olivia. Insofar as she fails in this task by causing Olivia to bestow love on the servant instead of the master, she has betrayed her master; but insofar as she succeeds, she has betrayed her own newly awakened love for him. Whatever Viola does in the role of Cesario must work against her interests in some sense and at some level, a fact that helps to explain an often-noted passivity in her character:

> A blank, my lord; she never told her love,
> But let concealment like a worm i' the bud
> Feed on her damask cheek; she pin'd in thought,
> And with a green and yellow melancholy

> She sate like Patience on a monument,
> Smiling at grief.
>
> (II.iv.110–15)

It would obviously be an error to take Viola's displaced version of herself as the final word about her character: she is, after all, capable of vigorous action.[7] And yet a comparison with Rosalind's merrily cynical versions of herself will suggest that there is something genuinely sad about Viola's double bind, something that can only be resolved, if at all, by the impersonal agencies of time and fortune. If Rosalind can choose the time to resolve her situation (when she has brought Orlando to avow, "I can live no longer by thinking" [V.ii.50]), Viola must simply await the resolution of hers. "What else may hap, to time I will commit" (I.ii.60): "O time, thou must untangle this, not I, / It is too hard a knot for me t' untie" (II.ii.40–41).

Disguise, language, time: the last is the ultimately recalcitrant means, the most elusive and willful mediation the play offers, the agency in no way subject to the desires of human beings, and yet in the end the only force for resolving the complications the plot has generated. It is thus hardly surprising that those characters in *Twelfth Night* less wise than Viola (and even she shuttles between patient resignation and active intervention) spend considerable energy attempting to use in one way or another the first two means, disguise and language, to control or modify or oppose the last, which is finally only in an illusory sense a means available to human beings at all. The struggle with time is played out in *Twelfth Night* in a variety of registers, but in each case we can glimpse at the heart of it the sympathetic and altogether understandable (if inevitably frustrated) wish to deny the fact of one's own death. But if the thought of death is banished from the comic world, it always returns, a process of which Feste's first song (II.iii) appears to be a paradigm. If the first stanza insists that "Journeys end in lovers meeting" (43), the last subjoins a rueful reflection:

> What's to come is still unsure.
> In delay there lies no plenty,
> Then come kiss me sweet and twenty;
> Youth's a stuff will not endure.
>
> (49–52)

It is perhaps in the first great exchange between Viola as Cesario and Olivia (I.v) that we can glimpse most clearly the poignancy at the heart of all Illyrian foolery. The measure of Viola's quick wit and insight is the speed

with which she responds to Olivia's rather uncourteous haughtiness and
parries it: "The rudeness that hath appear'd in me have I learn'd from my
entertainment" (I.v.214–15). But the measure of something even deeper
than wit and insight, a kind of imaginative intuition, is Viola's ability to
grasp Olivia's haughtiness as a defense, a way of refusing certain truths
about mutability and decay. When Viola first sees Olivia's face, her appre-
ciation of her womanly beauty is genuine:

> 'Tis beauty truly blent, whose red and white
> Nature's own sweet and cunning hand laid on.
> Lady, you are the cruell'st she alive
> If you will lead these graces to the grave,
> And leave the world no copy.
>
> (I.v.239–43)

Viola's mention of the grave reminds us that Olivia has been recently be-
reaved of both a father and a brother. In seasoning "a brother's dead love"
(I.i.29–30) she is really denying the fact of his death and with that the inevitability of her own. In giving the world a "copy" of her beauty (in Viola's
sense) she would be recognizing the certainty of her own demise by a process
common in Shakespeare's work in which the appearance of a new generation makes the old acutely aware of its own mortality. It is precisely this
awareness that Olivia deflects by taking Viola's "copy" to mean "schedule"
or "record." The implications of what Viola has said to her she is unprepared
to hear.

"Beauty's a flower," Feste has reminded Olivia in his first appearance earlier in this same scene (52), a remark echoed when Orsino later says to Viola, "For women are as roses, whose fair flow'r / Being once display'd, doth
fall that very hour" (II.iv.38–39). Viola's response, "And so they are; alas,
that they are so! / To die, even when they to perfection grow!" (40–41), reveals not only her grasp of mortality, but the poignancy of her own inability
to seize romantic opportunity, her sense that as long as she is in disguise, she
is not only wasting time but time is wasting her. It is this repressed awareness that we sense in Olivia in I.v, in her curious way of putting herself at a
distance ("Speak to me, I shall answer for her" [168}), in the brittle quality
of her diction in general, perhaps most of all in her comparison of herself to
a painted portrait: "but we will draw the curtain, and show you the picture.
Look you, sir, such a one I was this present. *Unveiling.* Is't not well done?"
(233–35). Viola's rather arch rejoinder ("Excellently done, if God did all")
provokes Olivia's assertion, "'Tis in grain, sir, 'twill endure wind and

weather" (237–38). But we sense that the reason Olivia compares her face to a work of art is that a work of art does not change, and it is precisely change that she fears. Indeed, "wind and weather" (and Feste's concluding song reminds us that "the rain it raineth every day" [V.i.392]) are precisely what Olivia cannot endure.

Olivia is an extreme (if, in the circumstances, understandable) example of a dialogue with time and mutability that underlies virtually all of the foolery in *Twelfth Night*. Even at the height of merry inconsequence, we glimpse a certain urgency subtending the revelry, as in Sir Toby's sophistical argument concerning the timely taking of rest: "To be up after midnight and to go to bed then, is early; so that to go to bed after midnight is to go to bed betimes" (II.iii.7–9). Such choplogic and wordplay are Toby's way of denying the passage of time, or at least of seeing it as a beneficent cycle rather than as a one-way trip to oblivion. His equivocation on the word "early" is analogous to Olivia's on the word "copy," and, however we may see Olivia as ultimately sympathetic, Toby as comically grandiose, both attempt, by purely linguistic means, to fend off the wind and the rain.

Of all the people of *Twelfth Night* perhaps only the clown Feste is in firm possession from first to last of the fact that language cannot change the structure of reality. Although he is the greatest "corrupter of words" in the play (as he calls himself in his single exchange with Viola [III.i.36]), his equivocations have a satiric edge, as if he were mocking those who are under the delusion that they can control reality with language. As he says to Viola of his sister and his wish that she had no name, "Why, sir, her name's a word, and to dally with that word might make my sister wanton" (III.i.19–20). His way of citing nonexistent authorities ("Quinapalus" [I.v.35], "Pigrogromitus" [II.iii.23], "the old hermit of Prague" [IV.ii.12–13]) seems undertaken in the same fey spirit. It is ultimately a demonstration that language cannot conjure, however much we may wish it could—if it is not (as it may well be) an unsettling suggestion that all authority is finally an effect of language. How do we know in the end, Feste's citation of nonexistent authorities seems to ask, that Homer and Vergil and Saint Augustine, for instance, existed, but Quinapalus and the old hermit of Prague did not? The evidence for the existence of the first three is purely circumstantial, a matter of the texts attributed to them and the testimony of contemporaries. How do we really know that the *Aeneid* of Vergil was not written by one Quinapalus calling himself "Vergil"? Feste calls himself "Sir Topas," and Malvolio accepts the identification without cavil (IV.ii.21–24). We are all in Malvolio's "dark room and bound" (III.iv.135–36) to this extent.

This is not to say that language is altogether impotent in *Twelfth Night*, but to begin to see that its powers are not always what the speaker thinks they are, much less always under his control. Truly committing ourselves to language is something like committing ourselves to another in a love relationship: it implies the risk of being misunderstood or rejected or erased by the logic of the other, whether understood as another person or the structure of language itself. If a language held in common is a means to social unity, it can also become, wittingly or unwittingly, comically divisive, a source of disruption. We saw in the last chapter that meaning is stabilized and made univocal by the rigorous exclusion of other possible meanings, which nevertheless have a way of returning from the margins of discourse.[8] I may now add that meaning in language is never the exclusive property of the individual speaker, for it is determined by a transpersonal consensus of the linguistic community.[9] Our words are neither our property (in the double sense of "belongings" and "essence"), nor the property of a single other—a salient fact Malvolio overlooks in assuming that the forged letter must have come from Olivia. With language as with love we are as much possessed as we are in possession, either of our words or of ourselves, a condition Olivia discovers as she is smitten by "Cesario": "Fate, show thy force: ourselves we do not owe; / What is decreed must be; and be this so" (I.v.310–11).

It is perhaps an anxious intuition of the truth Olivia tumbles to in the process of falling in love that causes in the gloomy Malvolio something like what is known in psychoanalysis as "reaction-formation." Freud was led to suspect that certain recurrent clusters of traits he found in his patients were actually character formations aimed at denying or sublimating—in any case at controlling—various infantile desires still present in the individual but wholly unacceptable under prevailing standards of adult behavior. Thus the combination of orderliness, parsimony, and obstinacy seemed to Freud the individual's way of reacting against infantile anal erotism, the wish to play with dirt and to take pleasure in defecation.[10] We should be wary of treating Malvolio as a pathological type, and yet the strategy of denying by retreating into the opposite implicit in reaction-formation seems an illuminating approach to understanding Malvolio within the economy of *Twelfth Night,* for his rigidity in particular, along with a massive ego that would apparently absorb the whole world if it could, suggests an underlying fascination with (and a simultaneous fear of) dispersion and loss of identity, the conditions of the revelry and festivity he otherwise so furiously opposes.[11]

In Malvolio's disordered relation to language we can most readily grasp his overweening desire to control and order the situations in which he finds himself (it is not for nothing that such a personality becomes a steward). His stilted prose, full of inkhorn terms meticulously meted out, which is in one sense simply the sign of his pretentious ambition to rise in the world, is also the most eloquent testimony to the need to control:

> My masters, are you mad? Or what are you?
> Have you no wit, manners, nor honesty, but to gabble
> like tinkers at this time of night? Do ye make an
> alehouse of my lady's house, that ye squeak out your
> coziers' catches without any mitigation or remorse
> of voice? Is there no respect of place, persons, nor
> time in you?
>
> (II.iii.86–92)

The proliferation of terms ("wit, manners, honesty"; "mitigation or remorse"; "place, persons, nor time"), on one level mere lexical display, can be understood on another as a compulsive drive to leave no stone linguistically unturned, to catch all aspects of the situation in the net of language, to let no possibilities escape the controlling will.[12] Malvolio would make language quibble-proof. It thus seems comically appropriate that the man who began in attempting to master the world by language will end up mastered by it in his turn, as he falls prey to a cleverly forged but perhaps not altogether credible letter.[13] It seems further appropriate, if not comically so, that this same man mastered by language calls from his dark room for "ink, paper, and light" (IV.ii.109–10) in an attempt (which would be touching, if it were not so obtuse) to regain the upper hand. Malvolio would be better off, if, like Feste's old hermit of Prague, he "never saw pen and ink" (IV.ii.13).

Toby's cheeky rejoinder to Malvolio's diatribe in II.iii already figures the ultimate futility of attempting absolute control of language and through it of the self and world: "We did keep time, sir, in our catches. Sneck up!" (93–94). By equivocating on the sense of time as hour of the day and time as musical rhythm, Toby manages to destabilize Malvolio's rigid speech, to make it say, in effect, something the speaker has scarcely intended. While Malvolio is by no means the only one vulnerable to such linguistic divagation (we have already seen Viola at the outset in I.ii.54–55 producing a meaning she does not quite intend), it is perhaps clearest in his instance. His rigidly obsessive attitude constantly generates its antithesis, providing *Twelfth Night* with some of its more interesting paradoxes. If, on the one hand, Malvolio always sees himself as unique, as the embodiment of absolute difference ("Go hang yourselves all! You are idle shallow things, I am not of your element" [III.iv.123–24]), we, on the other hand, see him as constantly mirrored and duplicated in the characters and situations that involve him. ,

Indeed, Malvolio tries to master "the trick of singularity," to borrow Maria's apt and far-reaching phrase in the forged letter (II.v.151–52), and repeatedly fails in one way or another in the attempt. Although he thinks of himself as a thorough "original," the play is always revealing his origins, what is anterior to and determining of him. Thus his peculiarly constricted way of speaking, lest equivocation insinuate itself and frustrate his intention, turns out to derive from books, the effect of the fact that, as Maria points out, he "cons state without book, and utters it by great swarths" (II.iii.149), that is, he gets passages from his authors by heart and then utters them publically as if they were his own. Malvolio's distinguished speech does not really distinguish him, for it derives from a source anterior to the self. In his drive to embody difference he has made himself the creature of another's text, a situation nicely parodied by Viola in her first encounter with Olivia, when she pretends to be a young actor who must hew strictly to the part he has memorized with such pains: "I can say little more than I have studied, and that question's out of my part" (I.v.178–79). Viola is skillfully parrying Olivia's question about origins, "Whence came you, sir?" The question is not merely "out of" her part, for to answer it would destroy her part altogether: Viola preserves her adopted persona by feigning incompetence. Malvolio too suppresses origins, but with perfectly genuine incompetence and for rather different reasons. His strained effort to be what he can only in the end impersonate (by "practicing behavior to his own shadow" [II.v.17]) ends in the realization (ours, at least, if not his) that the identity he so laboriously constructs and feverishly defends is always elsewhere, always the property of others. Small wonder, then, that by insisting on what he thinks of as his "property" (in the sense of his distinguishing characteristics) he comes to be "propertied" in the dark room (IV.ii.91). There is an ironic sting in Olivia's discovery as it applies to Malvolio: "ourselves we do not owe."

It is clear that "property" in all its senses, along with the related ideas of possessing and possessions, having, holding, appropriating for the self and bestowing from it, is at the heart of the giddy swirl of foolery in *Twelfth Night*. To wish to possess in the romantic sense is to become possessed by the madness to which love is repeatedly compared; to hold the self in aloof reserve, as Olivia tries to do in her protracted mourning, is in a paradoxical way to lose it, for "beauty is a flower." "What is yours to bestow is not yours to reserve" (I.v.188–89), Viola-as-Cesario reminds her, and it is only in abandoning herself to romantic desire, in giving herself away to the force of fate and time that Olivia will achieve a truer understanding that the self is never singular but always plural, a construct of the social rather than a solitary being whose integrity is simply a given. Husbanding the self in the sense of keeping it in reserve must veer about into the antithetical sense of husbanding, that is, doubling in marriage.

"What is yours to bestow is not yours to reserve": Viola slyly suggests the paradox that what is kept back is not really ours and does not become truly ours until bestowed elsewhere. It is not only Viola's wisdom but the play as a whole that suggests that this business of giving the self away is not something the individual has much choice about. It happens, willy-nilly. This is not so much what Malvolio discovers as what we discover about him, for he remains in the dark even after his release from literal benightment. The trick of singularity, which he is so obsessively committed to mastering, is just that, an illusion and thus a trick played upon him rather than one that he can master. Malvolio is always giving himself away in the sense of unwittingly revealing himself, but he also gives himself away well and truly, losing himself to a part with which he has become so intensely engaged that he has lost all sense of it as a part. This is far enough from the joyful acquiescence of Olivia in losing herself and the inspired acting of Viola in which multiple parts are simultaneously played and yet kept separate that it seems to constitute a dark parody of them.

"O, peace! now he's deeply in," says Fabian as he watches Malvolio from the box-tree. "Look how imagination blows him" (II.v.42–43). Fabian's delighted exclamation suggests that Malvolio has abandoned himself to imagination (and note, Fabian does not say "his imagination"), to a fantasy of social domineering in which the self stands alone and commands absolutely. We have the rather sour paradox of a man playing without being in the least playful, of merry festivity in the guise of gloomy careerism. And if we look closely at Malvolio's fantasy of rising in the world to preeminence, it begins to seem strangely like the festive foolery he otherwise so stringently rejects, for it undertakes in a serious way exactly the kind of inversion of established social categories true foolery merely plays with as comic possibility, the kind of "uncrowning" of authority and authoritative structure associated with the carnivalesque in all its forms.[14] In rising from steward to lord and installing himself at the top of the social heap Malvolio would enact precisely the topsy-turvy "uncivil rule" with which he charges Sir Toby (II.iii.123).

He would also make the inversion permanent, freeze his new status by refusing all that is anterior to it and all that might supersede it in a kind of timeless fantasy that he repeatedly gives the specious look of divine ratification ("Jove and my stars be prais'd!" [II.v.172–73]):

> Seven of my people, with an obedient start,
> make out for him. I frown the while, and perchance
> wind up my watch, or play with my—some rich jewel.
> Toby approaches; curtsies there to me—
>
> (II.v.58–61)

The present tense here is an indication of how deeply Malvolio really is "in," but it also suggests the rigor with which he tries to repress time and the historical. And it is a measure of time's revenges that Malvolio verges on saying that he plays with his "chain," the very badge of his anterior status, before catching himself and substituting the vague "some rich jewel." It is remarkable throughout Malvolio's timeless fantasies how clearly we can still hear his watch ticking, for it measures the time that will finally wind him up in its turn. As Feste remarks at the conclusion, "And thus the whirligig of time brings in his revenges" (V.i.376–77).[15]

It is Malvolio's refusal of the topsy-turvy principle of reversal and table turning that links him most profoundly with Sir Toby, whom he ironically persists in seeing only as his greatest adversary. We have seen that Toby too tries to make life into a perpetual revel, to banish the everyday completely, an everyday that returns just as surely to him in the form of "a bloody coxcomb" (V.i.176) as it does to Malvolio in the form of his humiliation in the dark room. What both men ignore is the wisdom of Prince Hal in the first part of *Henry IV*:

> If all the year were playing holidays,
> To sport would be as tedious as to work;
> But when they seldom come, they wish'd for come,
> And nothing pleaseth but rare accidents.
>
> (I.ii.204–07)[16]

That we discover in Sir Toby, whom Malvolio thinks of as his pure opponent and opposite, a sort of repressed or hidden double is the strongest testimony to Malvolio's failure to work the trick of singularity.

The analogy, of course, cuts both ways: just as Toby's example shows up Malvolio's limitations, so Malvolio's example shows up Toby's. Toby's below-stairs roistering reaches no triumphant conclusion; it rather becomes increasingly pointless and finally fizzles out in the punishments the incensed

Sebastian visits on its principles. It is almost as if the everyday in the form of a man who really is a man underneath it all were taking its revenge on the one who would make all life a perpetual holiday. We have the sense in the last third of the play that Toby has overextended himself in working two parallel deceptions, the one on Malvolio, the other on the far more sympathetic Sir Andrew, who, though he is not long on brains, has nonetheless a fund of goodwill and even a kind of transient common sense. He is also Toby's double in that he is always echoing him ("I'll make one too"—the phrase amusingly suggests "I'll make one two"), and yet the occasional pathos of his character may make us slightly uneasy about his victimization, especially when we consider that it is specifically motivated (in a way true foolery never is) by the desire to extort money. "Pleasure will be paid, one time or another," Feste has said to Orsino (II.iv.70–71), but there seems no good reason in Toby's case why Andrew should be left to pick up the check.

The suspicion that revelry is overextended in the last third of *Twelfth Night* helps to explain the fact that for many students of the play such uneasiness as they may feel with the bilking of Sir Andrew tips over into downright discomfort and dismay with the upshot of the gulling of Malvolio. Ralph Berry has recently called the dark room sequence "theatre as blood sport" and is driven to conclude that "the ultimate effect of *Twelfth Night* is to make the audience ashamed of itself."[17] This is undoubtedly an extreme position, and yet it has the merit of focusing a certain queasiness that cannot really be dismissed as the result of historical shifts in sensibility or taste. Malvolio really is, to use a phrase later echoed by Olivia, "notoriously abus'd" (IV.ii.87–88).

The nature of the abuse here bears some scrutiny, for what the pranksters abuse is in the largest sense the theatrical means at their disposal. One of the conceivable ways of understanding Feste's tautologies ("'That that is is'; so I, being Master Parson, am Master Parson" [IV.ii.14–15]) is by grounding them in the conditions that obtain during a theatrical performance, where actors "are" for the duration the characters they portray. But the conditions of theater are fully as fragile as the conditions of true festivity. It takes very little to topple a theatrical illusion and reveal it for what it "is" in another sense—an assembly of men pretending to be what they manifestly are not—just as it takes very little for a merry prank to gain a hard edge of aggression and revenge. There are numerous instances in Shakespeare's plays where the playwright himself calls attention to the fragility of his illusion, as in *Twelfth Night* itself when Fabian remarks of Malvolio's outlandish behavior, "If this were play'd upon a stage now, I could condemn it as an improbable fiction" (III.iv.127–28). The remark restores to full view the theatrical machinery underlying the whole play, but it also reminds us of the extent to which we can choose to give assent to the proceedings in hand or withhold it.'

Malvolio in the dark room, on the other hand, is deprived of precisely this freedom and at a considerable disadvantage, for darkness drastically reduces the means of reality testing otherwise available to the spectator at a theatrical performance. And it is only within this narrowed context that Feste can approach "being" Master Parson. In the dark room episode we may easily suspect that the theatrical experience has been unfairly rigged to exclude the context that questions it and with which it must normally establish a dialogue. Sealed off in this way from reality it is free to go where it will, to take over rather in the way Toby would have the festive in general take over to the exclusion of the mundane.[18] But as with disguise, the tendency for means to become ends has a way of turning on those who would use them. It is finally as if the pranksters have been caught in the logic of their prank, an effect underscored by Toby's oddly passive remark, "I would we were well rid of this knavery" (IV.ii.67–68). Such comic mood as there may have been has obviously soured.

Insofar as the dark room episode can be understood as a means of educating Malvolio about himself, and thus as something more than a vengeful joke, it seems aimed at his illusory view of character as unified and integral. The recurrent metaphor of demonic possession that Feste adopts in addressing him ("Out, hyperbolical fiend! how vexest thou this man! Talkest thou nothing but of ladies?" [IV.ii.25–26]) is a way of expressing the very doubleness Malvolio would deny in himself. In suggesting that Malvolio does not so much speak as that an alien voice speaks in him, the fool touches on the essence not only of Malvolio's condition but on that of Olivia and Orsino, who have internalized their chosen roles to the point of losing sight of them, and finally on that of the theatrical event itself, where actors are "possessed" by selves and language not of their own making. It is perhaps to this sense of the theatrically doubled self that Feste speaks in questioning Malvolio about "the opinion of Pythagoras" (50), for Pythagorean transmigration of souls is a kind of philosophical equivalent of theatrical doubling, and Malvolio's rejection of it is evidence of his refusal to allow that entities interpenetrate and interchange in the harmonious reciprocity that marks the true lovers at the conclusion of *Twelfth Night*.

No matter how we experience the tone of the joke played on Malvolio, however, the fact remains that insofar as it is aimed at bringing him to his senses and giving him a more workable sense of the self, it is a failure. He remains in willful isolation to the end, and his exit line promising "revenge on the whole pack" (V.i.378), those who have conspired against him as well as those who have not, suggests a failure in the comic wholly to contain the cycle of revenge and counterrevenge that in another kind of play would become the basis for a thoroughly tragic vision. This is not, however, to deny *Twelfth Night* comic status on Malvolio's sole account, but to realize that Shakespeare has here arranged for a comic structure to suggest its own limits.[19] This journey does, after all, end in lovers' meeting, at least for those willing to abandon a rigid and isolating conception of the self. When the twins are at last united in the final scene and reality itself seems to double and pun, we are brought to realize that true mutuality in love can only consist in being at once possessing and possessed.

There remains, of course, the question of agency. I remarked at the beginning that the comic resolution of *Twelfth Night* is finally brought about not by human will but by the mysterious workings of what is variously called "Time" or "Fate" or "Fortune." When Feste sums up the subplot in saying "And thus the whirligig of time brings in his revenges" (V.i.376–77), he provokes the realization that in the action he speaks of it is precisely not the impersonal agency of time that has brought about a conclusion, successful or unsuccessful, but human contrivance.[20] Time seems to have had nothing to do with it. And yet even this formulation seems a trifle too strong. Time has had nothing to do with the revenge on Malvolio, but surely Toby's bloody coxcomb is the result of Sebastian's chance wandering on the scene at precisely the right moment. Even in the subplot time and human contrivance seem simultaneously at work.

Feste's remark has a complicated effect, for while it reinforces our sense of impersonal forces working in the main plot (by comically locating them in the part of the subplot from which they are conspicuously absent), it also reminds us of a human artificer who stands behind not just one or another plot but behind the whole of the dramatic fiction that is *Twelfth Night,* the playwright himself. This does not mean, however, that the play we have just witnessed is simply a contrivance to be dismissed as sheer artifice or merely a trick. That would be to take an excessively singular view of what the playwright is up to in submitting himself to the manifold risks of the theatrical enterprise, balancing his contrivance against the whims of taste and fashion, his view of what the play should be against the views of the actors who will perform it, anticipating a play's reception or responding to it. Even when we speculate on the nature of the artistic problems Shakespeare faced, it would seem, the trick of singularity is difficult to work.

# Conclusion

We cannot in the circumstances know precisely why Shakespeare abandoned the comic genre just after the turn of the seventeenth century, never to take it up again in its pure form. It is certainly not the case that after *Measure for Measure* (1604), the last play classified as a comedy, he never again wrote a funny line, for even the tragedies, notoriously, contain comic passages (though calling them "comic relief" has been thoroughly discredited), and the four final plays, now classified as the "Late Romances," have abundant passages of high fun.[1] *The Tempest* (1611), in all probability the last work entirely by Shakespeare, has some very funny moments of inspired fooling. It is thus clearly not the case that Shakespeare suddenly and mysteriously lost his sense of humor around 1604, nor does the theory of a period of depression, a change in his fundamental mood, seem altogether compelling. Morose people have written comedies, after all, and one supposes cheerful people have written tragedies. Saying that comedies cannot proceed except from a mood of elation is a little like saying one cannot write a poem about winter during the warm months. There may be in some instances such correlations, but they are neither necessary nor inevitable.

Perhaps Shakespeare abandoned comedy simply because he thought he had exhausted its potential as far as his particular talent was concerned. It is a restrictive genre, after all, binding the author to certain well-established protocols, and, as Northrop Frye remarks, it "has been remarkably tenacious of its structural principles and character types." Frye goes on to remind us of G. B. Shaw's only half-joking remark that "a comic artist could get a reputation for daring originality by stealing his method from Molière and his characters from Dickens: if we were to read Menander and Aristophanes for Molière and Dickens the statement would hardly be less true, at least as a general principle."[2] Even in the work coming before the problem plays the sense of strain is often evident, as a certain skepticism about the efficacy of comic action makes itself felt. We may leave *Much Ado about Nothing,* for instance, wondering whether experience has really changed the inner life of the likes of Claudio and Don Pedro, and for many no amount of talk about conventional churls and killjoys will ever make them entirely easy with the treatment of Malvolio in *Twelfth Night*. The resolutions of the later comedies tend to be increasingly partial, and the marriages that are the traditional sign of festive atonement seem grudgingly included only because they are what comic protocol demands. Of the three projected marriages that mark the conclusion of *Measure for Measure,* two amount to judicial sentences for the male characters, while the third is so unexpected that the prospective bride is apparently stricken dumb. Certainly no one would fault the finale of *Measure for Measure* on grounds of excessive festivity.

We may be sure at least that Shakespeare did not abandon writing comedy for the stage because he found the genre trivial or merely amusing. There was and still is a common prejudice that what is funny in literature is only that and must therefore lack depth or seriousness. In the nineteenth century Matthew Arnold excluded Chaucer from the ranks of the greatest English poets because he seemed to Arnold to lack "high seriousness," a judgment that today seems not only priggish but simply wrong.[3] Shakespeare could not have understood his own comic work as trivial or lacking in depth, and wherever his comic genius expresses itself we can be sure that he is using laughter to bring a fresh perspective to a serious problem. It is a widespread recognition of this fact that may be the reason for the lapse of the notion of comic relief in tragedy as a useful analytic category. We cannot understand the Fool's function in *King Lear,* for instance, as merely providing flashes of amusement in an otherwise harrowing story. His remarks are simply too pointed or poignant or moving (though they may be funny as well) to dismiss as "relief." Indeed, they do much to intensify the spectacle of the great king's gradual reduction to "the thing itself," "unaccommodated man," "a poor, bare, fork'd animal" (III.iv.106–08), raving mad and wandering the stormy heath.

There are, to be sure, such things as trivial comedies (there are trivial tragedies too), but it is certain that Shakespeare wrote none of them. Even a play as apparently inconsequential as *The Merry Wives of Windsor,* though scarcely in the first rank of Shakespeare's comedies, will repay careful attention and analysis. Shakespearean comedy is an instrument for exploring some of the most crucial questions we face, and if they are not the same questions that tragedy explores, they are still worthy of putting if not easy to answer. What does it mean to be social? is one recurrent question, and it implies another: What does it mean to be solitary? We have seen Shakespeare repeatedly probing the dialectic of self and other, individual and collective, the one and the many, by means of comedy. Or again: How does the process of human growth and development work, and what can go wrong with it? If the romantic comedies are not at least partly about maturation, it is difficult to see how they can be about anything at all. No one will doubt that the Shakespearean comic catharsis and the recognition it brings have to do with growing awareness and self-consciousness, and it just may be that our first set of questions and the dialectic they imply are involved in a yet larger dialectic with our second set of questions, for surely the process of growing up involves becoming truly social, and yet being truly social is an important element in the process of growing up. Anyone who dismisses these questions as trivial also risks dismissing the complexity and richness of life itself.

# Notes and References

*Introduction*

1. *Poetics*, 1449 a 10; see *Aristotle's Theory of Poetry and Fine Art*, trans. S. H. Butcher (New York: Dover, 1951), 19.

2. Dudley Fitts has made some of the liveliest modern translations of Aristophanes; see *Aristophanes: Four Comedies*, trans. Dudley Fitts (New York: Harcourt Brace, 1954). The four comedies are the *Lysistrata*, the *Frogs*, the *Birds*, and the *Thesmophoriazusae*, which Fitts translates under the appropriate title of *Ladies' Day*.

3. For a succinct and penetrating account of the workings of the typical New Comedy, see Northrop Frye, "The Argument of Comedy," in *English Institute Essays 1948*, ed. D. A. Robertson, Jr. (New York: Columbia University Press, 1949), 58–73.

4. Menander was a student of the philosopher Theophrastus, author of the *Charakteres*, a treatise comprising 30 sketches of character types deviating from the proper norms of behavior. Theophrastus may have had a good deal of influence on Menander's view of comic character on the stage.

5. For a magisterial account of the history and development of Latin comedy, see George Duckworth, *The Nature of Roman Comedy* (Princeton: Princeton University Press, 1952). Erich Segal's more recent *Roman Laughter: The Comedy of Plautus* (Cambridge: Harvard University Press, 1968) is a fine overview and analysis of the elder statesman of Roman comedy.

6. Greene was also the author of an attack on Shakespeare in a pamphlet entitled *Groats-worth of witte* (1592). This is the earliest documentary evidence we have of Shakespeare at work as a playwright in London. The man responsible for its publication, Henry Chettle, subsequently published an apology; see *The Riverside Shakespeare*, appendix B, items 8 and 9.

7. For an excellent account of the fusion of traditions in this play, see David P. Young, *Something of Great Constancy: The Art of "A Midsummer Night's Dream"* (New Haven: Yale University Press, 1966), 9–60.

8. Robert Weimann, *Shakespeare and the Popular Tradition in the Theater: Studies in the Social Dimension of Dramatic Form and Function* (1967; rev. ed., Baltimore: Johns Hopkins University Press, 1978).

9. See the fourth volume of *A Select Collection of Old English Plays*, ed. W. Carew Hazlitt (London: Reeves and Turner, 1874), 159.

10. Northrop Frye, *Anatomy of Criticism: Four Essays* (Princeton: Princeton University Press, 1957), 172–75. The *Tractatus Coislinianus*, a late peripatetic document probably from the first century B.C., looks like an attempt to supplement

the *Poetics* by giving an Aristotelean view of comedy. It takes its name from the De Coislin Collection in the Bibliothèque Nationale at Paris, where the manuscript resides.

*Chapter One*

1. The tetralogy comprises the three plays dealing with the reign of Henry VI and *Richard III.*

2. For the pertinent passage, see appendix B, item 14 in *The Riverside Shakespeare.*

3. The scene where the two Dromios argue through the closed door of the Ephesian Antipholus's house (III.i) is obviously not in the *Menaechmi,* but Shakespeare borrowed it from another Plautine play where there are identical servants, the *Amphitruo.* Here and there he is indebted to still other sources, the tale of Apollonius of Tyre, for instance, for the long expositional story Egeon tells in the first scene. Shakespeare returns to this story in greater detail when he writes *Pericles* (1607–8) toward the end of his career.

4. Nevertheless, the romantic poet and theoretician Samuel Taylor Coleridge so concluded. He called the play "a legitimate farce in exactest consonance with the philosophical principles and character of farce, as distinguished from comedy and from entertainments"; see *Coleridge's Shakespearean Criticism,* 2 vols., ed. T. M. Raysor (Cambridge: Harvard University Press, 1930).

5. Robert B. Heilman, "Farce Transformed: Plautus, Shakespeare, and Unamuno," *Comparative Literature* 31, no. 2 (Spring 1979): 114.

6. Pascal remarks in his *Pensées,* "Two faces that are alike, although neither excites laughter by itself, make us laugh when together, on account of their likeness"; cited by Henri Bergson in his now classic treatise of risibility, *Laughter* (1900). Bergson's essay may be consulted in *Comedy,* ed. Wylie Sypher (Garden City, N.Y.: Doubleday, 1956), 61–190. The quotation from Pascal appears on page 82 of this edition.

7. Barry Weller makes the point that it is not so much "that Shakespeare was attentive to the intricacies of Pauline discourse," but that "in Paul's exposition of the Christian community [he] found a version of selfhood so overshadowed by the imperatives of solidarity that it represents a complete alternative and challenge to the selfhood which the character in search of definition hopes to achieve"; see "Identity and Representation in Shakespeare," *ELH* 49, no. 2 (Summer 1982): 346.

8. This kind of regression in the service of advancing is explored in a number of areas, including biological evolution, by Arthur Koestler in *The Ghost in the Machine* (New York: Macmillan, 1968). Koestler's view of the process is based on the French proverb *reculer pour mieux sauter,* draw back to leap forward.

9. And one result is that the audience knows from the start or quickly guesses the entire situation, while the characters remain ignorant of it up until the

very end. On this great gulf between audience awareness and that of the characters, see Bertrand Evans, *Shakespeare's Comedies* (Oxford: Clarendon Press, 1960), 3–9.

10. For an interesting account of the playwright as he is implicitly represented in the play, see Jonathan V. Crewe, "God or the Good Physician: The Rational Playwright in *The Comedy of Errors*," *Genre* 15, nos. 1 and 2 (Spring–Summer 1982): 203–23.

11. The process described here is doubtless an example of what Bergson calls "reciprocal interference of series"; see *Laughter*, 123–27.

12. The uninitiated but curious reader will find this oddity explained in *The Life and Opinions of Tristram Shandy, Gentleman*, ed. James Aiken Work (New York: Odyssey Press, 1940), 376–78. The incurious reader will simply have to take it on faith that there is, indeed, an explanation.

13. W. Thomas MacCary "*The Comedy of Errors:* A Different Kind of Comedy," *New Literary History* 9, no. 3 (Spring 1978): 525–36.

14. See Frye's essay "The Argument of Comedy," 58–59. Freud first elaborated his theory of the Oedipus complex in *The Interpretation of Dreams* (1900); see *The Standard Edition of the Complete Psychological Works of Sigmund Freud*, 24 vols. ed. James Strachey, trans. James Strachey et al. (London: Hogarth Press and the Institute of Psychoanalysis, 1953–74), vols. 4 and 5. All subsequent references to the works of Freud are keyed to this edition, hereafter cited as *S.E.*

15. MacCary's argument thus joins a revisionist movement in the psychoanalysis of recent years, the "object relations school," which stresses the importance of pre-oedipal relations. For a central document in this approach, see Margaret S. Mahler, Fred Pine, and Anni Bergman, *The Psychological Birth of the Human Infant: Symbiosis and Individuation* (New York: Basic Books, 1975).

16. The same is true of *The Tempest*, Shakespeare's other classically "correct" play. There Prospero must fill in the background of what is to ensue under the guise of telling his daughter that part of his and her history she is unable to remember; see I.ii.36–174.

17. See "The 'Uncanny'" in *S.E.* 17: 217–52.

18. Ibid., 235. Freud refers here to Rank's essay of 1914, "Der Doppelgänger," which appeared in the third volume of *Imago*. For an English translation, see *The Double: A Psychoanalytic Study*, trans. Harry Tucker, Jr. (Chapel Hill: University of North Carolina Press, 1971).

19. "The 'Uncanny,'" 236.

20. For an altogether fascinating account of this strategy and many others, see James L. Calderwood, *Shakespeare and the Denial of Death* (Amherst: University of Massachusetts Press, 1987).

*Chapter Two*

1. For an eloquent account of the high role of women as civilizers in Western comedy, see the English novelist George Meredith's *On the Idea of Comedy and of the Uses of the Comic Spirit* (1877) in *Comedy*, ed. Wylie Sypher, 3–57.

2. The standard, if rather uncritical, explication of these analogies as they form an encompassing and consistent worldview is E. M. W. Tillyard's *The Elizabethan World Picture* (London: Chatto and Windus, 1943). Most contemporary scholars view with considerable skepticism the unanimous consent to this ideological way of ordering important realities implied in Tillyard's argument.

3. A persuasive pursuit of this line of reasoning is Robert B. Heilman's "The 'Taming' Untamed; or, The Return of the Shrew," *Modern Language Quarterly* 27 (1966): 147–61.

4. The phrase in quotation marks is from Marianne L. Novy's fine essay "Patriarchy and Play in *The Taming of the Shrew*," *English Literary Renaissance* 9, no. 2 (Spring 1979): 264–80.

5. On the parallel between Sly and Kate as it bears on audience involvement, see Maynard Mack, "Engagement and Detachment in Shakespeare's Plays," in *Essays on Shakespeare and Elizabethan Drama in Honor of Hardin Craig,* ed. Richard Hosley (Columbia: University of Missouri Press, 1962), particularly 279–80.

6. For an intriguing study of theater as a form of metamorphosis in *The Taming of the Shrew* and other Shakespearean comedies, see William C. Carroll, *The Metamorphoses of Shakespearean Comedy* (Princeton: Princeton University Press, 1985).

7. Novy, "Patriarchy and Play in *The Taming of the Shrew*," 271.

8. Ibid., 271

9. Indeed, Richard Burt has recently argued that such harmony as there is between Petruchio and Kate is the effect of the presence of outsiders against whom the couple can join forces. "The resolution," Burt suggests, "does not put an end to social tensions and conflicts between characters, but keeps certain conflicts open in order to close others down"; see "Charisma, Coercion, and Comic Form in *The Taming of the Shrew*," *Criticism* 26, no. 4 (Fall 1984): 295–311. The quotation above is on page 304.

10. It can be argued cogently that *The Two Gentlemen of Verona* is Shakespeare's very first attempt to write for the stage; see Anne Barton's headnote to the play in *The Riverside Shakespeare,* 144.

11. See Janet Adelman's discussion of the play in "Male Bonding in Shakespeare's Comedies," in *Shakespeare's "Rough Magic": Renaissance Essays in Honor of C. L. Barber,* ed. Peter Erickson and Coppélia Kahn (Newark: University of Delaware Press, 1985), 76–79.

12. W. Thomas MacCary, *Friends and Lovers: The Phenomenology of Desire in Shakespearean Comedy* (New York: Columbia University Press, 1985), 94.

13. Howard Nemerov, *Poetry and Fiction: Essays* (New Brunswick, N.J.: Rutgers University Press, 1963), 29.

14. John F. Danby remarks of this comedy, "The processes of change in the characters, or in their mutual relations, are never lived through, only announced"; see "Shakespeare Criticism and *The Two Gentlemen of Verona*," *Critical Quarterly* 2,

no. 4 (Winter 1960): 316. It could be argued that Shakespeare soon learned to control and exploit this effect. The startling scene in *Romeo and Juliet* (1595) where the members of the Capulet household lament over what they take to be the corpse of Juliet (IV.v), for instance, is written in an old-fashioned declamatory style quite unlike anything else in the play.

15. For an account of the pervasive "textualization" of character in *The Two Gentlemen of Verona,* see Jonathan Goldberg, *Voice Terminal Echo: Postmodernism and English Renaissance Texts* (New York: Methuen, 1986), 68–100.

16. Alexander Leggatt remarks, "Love depends for its expression . . . on the sort of verbal cleverness that can actually detach the speaker from his feelings. It depends on words, and words are (like Launce and Speed) unreliable servants" (*Shakespeare's Comedy of Love* [London: Methuen, 1974], 30).

17. In his 1592 pamphlet *Groats-worth of witte, bought with a million of Repentance,* Robert Greene, with bad temper and worse grace, enjoins his fellow poets to quit the writing of plays and shun the actors in favor of "better Maisters; for it is pittie men of such rare wits, should be subiect to the pleasure of such rude groomes." We here glimpse something of the playwright's resentment of a situation that forces him to depend on others to embody his work before the public. Shakespeare's implied view of the matter may be said to contain something of this resentment, but it is characteristically far broader, more serene, and inclusive, covering, among many other things, both the author's and the actor's points of view. See the excerpt from Greene's pamphlet included in *The Riverside Shakespeare.*

18. Evidence for court performance comes from the title page of the First Quarto (Q1) of 1598, which says that the play was "presented before her Highnes this last Christmas." This quarto was probably preceded by a "bad" quarto, no copy of which survives, since the title page further says that the play has been "Newly corrected and augmented." Q1 contains extensive evidence of revision, including lines such as IV.iii.292–314, in Berowne's celebrated "Promethean fire" speech, which are evidently first drafts.

19. Carroll's study, *The Great Feast of Languages in "Love's Labour's Lost"* (Princeton: Princeton University Press, 1976), is one of the best treatments of the play in recent years and has been especially valuable in restoring awareness of balance and tentativeness in the play's stance. The phrases in quotation marks appear on page 28 of Carroll's book.

20. Rosalie Colie has some exquisite observations on this closing in of time in her chapter on *Love's Labor's Lost* in *Shakespeare's Living Art* (Princeton: Princeton University Press, 1974), 31–50.

21. One of Puck's speeches in *A Midsummer Night's Dream,* the next comedy Shakespeare would write, clearly echoes Berowne's language here, but foretells a more conventional resolution of the comedy: "Jack shall have Jill; / Nought shall go ill" (III.ii.461–62).

22. We do it, of course, by studying "three years," the words themselves rather than the duration they refer to, though Moth ends up accomplishing the feat

in considerably less than an hour. A logician would say this shift involves the "use / mention distinction." For a fine study of the many ways Shakespeare contrives to render the verbal medium opaque in this play, see James L. Calderwood, *Shakespearean Metadrama: The Argument of the Play in "Titus Andronicus," "Love's Labour's Lost," "Romeo and Juliet," "A Midsummer Night's Dream," and "Richard II"* (Minneapolis: University of Minnesota Press, 1971), 52–84.

23. Freud discusses this function of play in *Beyond the Pleasure Principle, S.E.* 18: 14–17.

24. Thomas M. Greene remarks cogently, "Berowne's teasing dilettantism is not up to death—nor (more surprisingly?) is it up to sex." Given what is ultimately at stake, it is not difficult to see why this should be so. See "*Love's Labour's Lost: The Grace of Society,*" *Shakespeare Quarterly* 22, no. 4 (Autumn 1971): 320.

25. Terence Hawkes has argued that the lords' progress can be measured by the fact that they finally reject the written and bookish in favor of the fully social mode of oral conversation. His argument relies on Plato's rejection of written discourse in the *Phaedrus.* See "Shakespeare's Talking Animals," *Shakespeare Survey* 24 (1971): 47–54.

26. The displacement inherent in the lords' ridicule has been previously noted, by both Alexander Leggatt and Thomas M. Greene, for instance. Greene remarks, "Indeed only the savage shame one feels toward an unworthy part of one's self could motivate the gentlemen's quite uncharacteristic cruelty"; see "*Love's Labor's Lost: The Grace of Society,*" 323. Leggatt's pertinent remarks may be found in *Shakespeare's Comedy of Love,* page 80. Neither critic proceeds to identify such scapegoating as a pervasive pattern in the play.

27. Even in his celebrated "Promethean fire" speech (IV.iii.286–362), as C. L. Barber noted, Berowne is still not "concerned with love as an experience between two people. All his attention is focussed on what happens within the lover, the heightening of his powers and perceptions"; see *Shakespeare's Festive Comedy: A Study of Dramatic Form and Its Relation to Social Custom* (1959; rpt., Princeton: Princeton University Press, 1972), 106.

*Chapter Three*

1. *The Diary of Samuel Pepys,* 2 vols., ed. Henry B. Wheatley (New York: Random House, 1946), 1:483.

2. From the "Induction" to *Bartholomew Fair,* ed. Eugene M. Waith (New Haven: Yale University Press, 1963).

3. *The Yale Edition of the Works of Samuel Johnson,* 15 vols. ed. E. L. McAdam, Jr. (New Haven: Yale University Press, 1958–78), 7:62. The seventh and eighth volumes are separately subtitled *Johnson on Shakespeare,* and will hereafter be cited by this title.

4. Ibid., 62.

5. The phrase in quotation marks is Ben Jonson's, from his "Dedicatory Verses" to the First Folio of 1623.

6. It is generally agreed that Shakespeare's play was originally designed to celebrate a noble wedding or weddings, but there is less agreement about which noble wedding. Perhaps the favorite candidate is that of William Stanley, earl of Derby, to Elizabeth Vere, daughter of the earl of Oxford. This wedding took place on 26 January 1595 at Greenwich Palace, a date that suits well with other evidence for the date of the play, which is usually reckoned 1595–96.

7. Kenneth Burke seems to be getting at the movement from form to theme when he remarks that "the artist's means are always tending to become ends in themselves"; see *Counter-Statement* (New York: Harcourt, Brace, 1931), 69.

8. The idea that works of literature are ultimately about themselves has become something of an irritating cliché of postmodernist criticism. In pointing to the reflexiveness of *A Midsummer Night's Dream*, I am not trying to suggest that the play is only about itself, or even that it is mainly preoccupied with itself. This kind of reflexiveness in drama has acquired the cumbersome if serviceable label "metadrama." One of the pioneering and most interesting forays into the metadramatics of Shakespeare's theater is James L. Calderwood's *Shakespearean Metadrama*, cited in the previous chapter in connection with *Love's Labor's Lost*. For a wry and penetrating critique of the notion of Shakespeare the Bard as the ultimate cultural signifier, see Malcolm Evans, *Signifying Nothing: Truth's True Contents in Shakespeare's Text* (Athens: University of Georgia Press, 1986).

9. Bradley's central work is the collection of lectures entitled *Shakespearean Tragedy* (London: Macmillan, 1904). L. C. Knights's cogent and now classic challenge to the characterological approach, "How Many Children Had Lady Macbeth?," first appeared in 1933 and was reprinted in modified form in his *Explorations* (London: Chatto and Windus, 1946), 1–39. Recently Jonathan Goldberg has put the matter about fictional character succinctly: "'Ourselves we do not owe' [the quotation is Olivia speaking in *Twelfth Night*]: character is construction, a social and textual production"; see "Textual Properties," *Shakespeare Quarterly* 37, no. 2 (Summer 1986): 217.

10. "The Plot, then, is the first principle, and, as it were, the soul of tragedy: Character holds the second place. . . . Thus tragedy is the imitation of an action, and of the agents mainly with a view to the action" (*Poetics*, 1450 a 37–38; *Aristotle's Theory of Poetry and Fine Art*, 27–29). Strictly speaking, Aristotle has no term that is the equivalent of "role," although the concept is clearly implied in his argument.

11. The term "blocking character" was devised by Northrop Frye to describe the authority of the older generation that thwarts the desires of the younger. For Frye's description of the typical plot structure of romantic comedy and a description of the typical characters inhabiting that plot, see *Anatomy of Criticism*, 163–86.

12. For a penetrating analysis of the problem of character and identity in *A Midsummer Night's Dream*, see Barry Weller's deft essay "Identity Dis-figured: *A Midsummer Night's Dream*," *Kenyon Review* 7, n.s., no. 3 (Summer 1985): 66–78.

13. *A Midsummer Night's Dream* is one of the few plays in the canon for

which it seems impossible to find a single main source. No one doubts, however, that, among the many literary influences operating in the text, Ovid's *Metamorphoses* ranks high in importance. The story of Pyramus and Thisbe, hilariously mangled by Peter Quince's company in the play-within-the-play is, of course, told by Ovid in his fourth book, although Shakespeare, perhaps significantly, has the hempen homespuns omit the concluding metamorphosis of Ovid's version.

14. For a consideration of various kinds of patterning emerging from the turns of the wooing game, see David P. Young, *Something of Great Constancy,* 61–108.

15. Cf. *Hamlet* I.i.13, where Barnardo calls Horatio and Marcellus "the rivals of my watch," that is, not the men who are vying with him for the right to stand guard, but those who will assist him in doing so. The word's Latin etymon, *rivalis,* means one sharing with another the right to use a stream, suggesting one who might be, but is not necessarily, in an adversarial relationship with a counterpart. There is a related antithesis in the English preposition "with." "I fight with my brother" may mean either that I fight on his side or against him. Only context can fully disambiguate the meaning.

16. Cf. Malvolio in the "dark house" in *Twelfth Night,* complaining of his tormentors: "They have here propertied me, keep me in darkness, send ministers to me, asses, and do all they can to face me out of my wits" (IV.ii.91–93).

17. For an extended discussion of the impersonality of desire in *A Midsummer Night's Dream* and *Twelfth Night,* see Terry Eagleton, *William Shakespeare* (Oxford: Basil Blackwell, 1986), 18–34.

18. This last explanation would make Demetrius's love for Hermia a true case of what René Girard has called "triangular desire," where one's desire for someone is always the result of the desire of another for the same person; see *Desire, Deceit, and the Novel,* trans. Yvonne Freccero (Baltimore: Johns Hopkins Press, 1965). For a consideration of "triangular" or "mimetic" desire in *A Midsummer Night's Dream* specifically, see Girard's essay, "Myth and Ritual in Shakespeare's *A Midsummer Night's Dream,*" in *Textual Strategies,* ed. Josue V. Harari (Ithaca: Cornell University Press, 1979), 189–212.

19. For an eloquent statement of Bottom's visionary power, see Frank Kermode, "The Mature Comedies," in *Early Shakespeare, Stratford-Upon-Avon Studies,* vol. 3, ed. John Russell Brown and Bernard Harris (New York: St. Martin's Press, 1961), 211–27.

20. Shakespeare continued to exploit the type of the character incapable of surprise throughout his comic writing. Thus Trinculo encounters the monstrous Caliban in *The Tempest* with something of the cool empiricism an organic chemist might bring to the qualitative analysis of an unknown substance:

> What have we here? a man or a fish? dead
> or alive? A fish, he smells like a fish;

> a very ancient and fish-like smell; a kind
> of not-of-the-newest poor-John. A strange fish!
> (II.ii.24–27)

21. *Johnson on Shakespeare*, 76.

22. See Anne Barton's introduction to the play in *The Riverside Shakespeare*, 217–21.

23. Shakespeare drew many of the details scattered throughout the play concerning Theseus's personal past from Plutarch's "Life of Theseus" in the 1579 translation of the *Lives* by Thomas North.

*Chapter Four*

1. For a historical overview of the theme of the three caskets and a provocative psychological explanation of it, see Freud's essay "The Theme of the Three Caskets" (1913), *S.E.* 12: 291–301.

2. For an example of such allegorical reading, see Nevill Coghill, "The Basis of Shakespearian Comedy: A Study in Medieval Affinities," in *Essays and Studies* (1950), 1–28.

3. Norman Rabkin devotes an introductory chapter to the controversies surrounding *The Merchant of Venice* and ends with an eloquent plea for a nonreductive criticism that respects contradictory responses; see *Shakespeare and the Problem of Meaning* (Chicago: University of Chicago Press, 1981), 1–32.

4. For the view of Shylock as conventional stage villain who relieves us of the need to accord him ordinary sympathy, see E. E. Stoll, *Shakespeare Studies, Historical and Comparative in Method* (New York: Macmillan, 1927), 255–336. For Shylock as victim of Venetian culture, see Terry Eagleton, *William Shakespeare*, 35–48.

5. Lawrence Danson, *The Harmonies of "The Merchant of Venice"* (New Haven: Yale University Press, 1978), 40.

6. Robert Ornstein, *Shakespeare's Comedies: From Roman Farce to Romantic Mystery* (Newark: University of Delaware Press, 1986), 93.

7. Marjorie Garber remarks of Shakespearean comedy that the "choice of false or intermediate objects of desire represents the middle stage in a progression from autoerotic to homoerotic and thence to fully adult, heterosexual, erotic identity"; see *Coming of Age in Shakespeare* (New York: Methuen, 1981), 142. For three cogent statements concerning rivalry between Antonio and Portia, see Graham Midgley, "*The Merchant of Venice*: A Reconsideration," *Essays in Criticism* 10, no. 2 (April 1960): 19–33; Lawrence W. Hyman, "The Rival Lovers in *The Merchant of Venice*," *Shakespeare Quarterly* 21, no. 2 (Spring 1970): 109–16; and Keith Geary, "The Nature of Portia's Victory: Turning to Men in *The Merchant of Venice*," *Shakespeare Survey* 37 (1984): 55–68.

8. For a penetrating analysis of male bonding in the early comedies, trage-

dies, and late romances, see Janet Adelman, "Male Bonding in Shakespeare's Comedies," *Shakespeare's "Rough Magic,"* 73–103.

9. The distinction between passive and active role-playing, the imposed role and the chosen, is discussed by Thomas F. Van Laan, *Role-Playing in Shakespeare* (Toronto: University of Toronto Press, 1978), 60–71.

10. On the obligations incurred by the receiver of a gift in primitive societies, see Marcel Mauss, *The Gift: Forms and Functions of Exchange in Archaic Societies* (*Essai sur le don*), trans. Ian Cunnison (New York: Norton, 1967). Mauss is particularly illuminating concerning the notion that the man who holds property through a gift is at once possessed of it and possessed by it, in that he becomes the creature of the imperative of restitution. The Roman institution of *nexum* ("binding," "tying together"), wherein the debtor pledged his liberty as forfeit, is reminiscent of Shylock's pound of flesh.

11. W. H. Auden, "Brothers and Others," in *The Dyer's Hand and Other Essays* (New York: Random House, 1962), 218–37.

12. There is a curious contradiction in what Antonio says here to Salerio and what he will say later in the scene to Bassanio: "Thou know'st that all my fortunes are at sea" (177). His apparently total ruin later in the play suggests that what he here tells Bassanio is correct, although there is still a suggestion, evident in all Antonio's dealings with his friend, of his tendency to present himself in extremity and thus as having a claim on Bassanio's attention and concern.

13. The effect may go beyond Portia's satiric portraits. As Alexander Leggatt remarks of Morocco, "he seems to have wandered into the wrong play"; see *Shakespeare's Comedy of Love,* 130. The peculiar expansiveness of his rhetoric as he contemplates making his choice of caskets (II.vii.39–47) might make one guess that he wanders in from Marlovian heroic tragedy, of which these lines seem a skillful parody.

14. For an illuminating discussion of Portia's championing of reciprocity in romantic relationships, see Marianne Novy, "Giving, Taking, and the Role of Portia in *The Merchant of Venice,*" *Philological Quarterly* 58, no. 2 (Spring 1979): 137–54.

15. Harry Berger, "Marriage and Mercifixion in *The Merchant of Venice,*" *Shakespeare Quarterly* 32, no. 2 (Summer 1981): 155–62.

16. "Sum of something" is the reading of the First Quarto, the copy-text for the Riverside edition. The First Folio has "sum of nothing," which yields a different but related meaning. The latter reading, in which we can hear "some of nothing," can be construed as Portia's way of qualifying her modesty, of asserting that she is only partially nothing.

17. This is essentially the point of view of Sigurd Burckhardt in his provocative study of *The Merchant of Venice,* "The Gentle Bond." Burckhardt also speculates that the real drama of the fourth act inheres in Portia's gradual discovery of a solution to the dilemma. We are not to assume that she enters the court with a pre-

conceived scenario in mind. See *Shakespearean Meanings* (Princeton: Princeton University Press, 1968), 206–36.

18. For an account of the threat of cuckoldry and Portia as an "unruly woman," see Karen Newman, "Portia's Ring: Unruly Women and Structures of Exchange in *The Merchant of Venice*," *Shakespeare Quarterly* 38, no. 1 (Spring 1987): 19–33.

## Chapter Five

1. The pertinent material is assembled by E. K. Chambers in *William Shakespeare: A Study of Facts and Problems,* 2 vols. (Oxford: Clarendon Press, 1930), 2: 261–66.

2. See Leslie Hotson, *Shakespeare versus Shallow* (Boston: Little, Brown, 1931), 111–22.

3. For a dissent from this view and a defense of the value of the play as a whole, see H. J. Oliver's introduction to the New Arden edition of *The Merry Wives of Windsor* (London: Methuen, 1971).

4. There is a possible exception in *The Comedy of Errors* with the marriage of Ephesian Antipholus and Adriana. But in that play domestic life plays a distinctly ancillary role to the main business of comic mistakings among the twin brothers and their twin servants.

5. For a detailed analysis of class and gender relations in this play, see Peter Erickson, "The Order of the Garter, the Cult of Elizabeth, and Class-Gender Tension in *The Merry Wives of Windsor*," in *Shakespeare Reproduced: The Text in History and Ideology,* ed. Jean E. Howard and Marion F. O'Connor (New York: Methuen, 1987), 116–40.

6. Northrop Frye perhaps did more than anyone to spark speculation about the ritual content of *The Merry Wives of Windsor.* For Frye the play contains "an elaborate ritual of the defeat of winter known to folklorists as 'carrying out Death.'"; see *Anatomy of Criticism,* 183. For an elaboration of the notion of Falstaff as ritual scapegoat, see Jeanne Addison Roberts, "*The Merry Wives of Windsor* as a Hallowe'en Play," *Shakespeare Survey* 25 (1972): 107–12.

7. One of the most intelligent and generous recent attempts to bolster this play's substance is William C. Carroll's, who remarks, "'Wit' is one of the chief agents of transformation, internal and external, and the stolid middle-class folk of Windsor will have none of it. Falstaff poses a threat to their rigid and comfortable social order, and such a threat to safely established boundaries cannot be tolerated"; see *The Metamorphoses of Shakespearean Comedy,* 186. If Falstaff had made the transition from history to comedy intact, I might be readier to accept this description of the threat he poses. But the Falstaff who uses a form letter in a seduction campaign is hardly very witty.

8. One of the best accounts of the effect of joining disparate modes of representation in *Much Ado about Nothing* can be found in Alexander Leggatt, *Shakespeare's Comedy of Love,* 151–83.

9. For a deft argument about the centrality of the act of communication in this play, see Anthony B. Dawson, "Much Ado about Signifying," *Studies in English Literature* 22, no. 2 (Spring 1982): 211–21.

10. Bertrand Evans discusses this anomaly and remarks, "Elsewhere, in comedies, histories, and tragedies alike, [Shakespeare's] way is to use Act I to lay the basis for the main action; nowhere else is there occasion for such surprise as is caused by the termination of the conflict between Claudio and the Prince"; see *Shakespeare's Comedies,* 72.

11. Evans is as vehement as anyone on the subject of Claudio, calling him the "most insufferable of Shakespeare's heroes of comedy, combining the hero's usual oblivion with priggish egocentricity," and remarking that his denunciation of Hero "has an exuberance that borders on sadism"; *Shakespeare's Comedies,* 80–81.

12. Freud, *Moses and Monotheism, S.E.* 23: 114.

13. For an illuminating analysis of this radically split image of women in the problem comedies, but with reference to *Much Ado about Nothing* and a good deal more of the canon as well, see Richard P. Wheeler, *Shakespeare's Development and the Problem Comedies: Turn and Counter-Turn* (Berkeley and Los Angeles: University of California Press, 1981). Freud's observations on this phenomenon, of which Wheeler makes extensive use, may be found in his essays on the psychology of love, "A Special Type of Choice of Object Made by Men" (1910), "On the Universal Tendency to Debasement in the Sphere of Love" (1912), and "The Taboo of Virginity" (1918), in *S.E.* 11: 163–208.

14. A. P. Rossiter astutely remarked of Beatrice and Benedick, "They fancy they are quite different *from,* and quite indifferent *to* each other. Indifferent they are not; and the audience is 'superior' in seeing their humours *as* humours; and in being aware that the opposite to love (as passionate, obsessive interest) is not hate (another passionate interest), but cool or unnoting indifference"; see *Angel with Horns and Other Shakespeare Lectures,* ed. Graham Storey (New York: Theatre Arts Books, 1961), 73. For an astute political and social argument about the play, though one that in my view concedes too much power and insight to Don Pedro in creating the relationship between Beatrice and Benedick, see Jean E. Howard, "Renaissance Antitheatricality and the Politics of Gender and Rank in *Much Ado about Nothing,"* in *Shakespeare Reproduced,* 163–87, particularly 177–78.

15. George Lyman Kittredge, ed., *The Complete Works of Shakespeare* (Boston: Ginn and Co., 1936). Cited by Anne Barton in a note to II.i.345 in *The Riverside Shakespeare.*

16. On the central role of fashion in *Much Ado about Nothing,* the "deformed thief" that is the subject of Borachio's rambling speech in III.iii, see John A. Allen's illuminating essay "Dogberry," *Shakespeare Quarterly* 24, no. 1 (Winter 1973): 35–53. Harry Berger, Jr., has made good use of Allen's insights and neatly articulated some truths about the limitations of male consciousness in this play in "Against the Sink-a-Pace: Sexual and Family Politics in *Much Ado about Nothing,"* *Shakespeare Quarterly* 33, no. 3 (Autumn 1982): 302–13.

17. Carol Cook has put the matter well from an informed feminist perspective: "Claudio's outburst against Hero has exposed the potential for cruelty and violence in Messina's masculine order so unequivocally that resolution would seem to depend on some kind of confrontation with the fears and assumptions of which Hero has been a victim. In the fiction of her death, however, the play finds a ritual resolution that reasserts Messina's stability without the need for painful questioning. Nonetheless, the play's attempt to move toward a comic conclusion and to evade what its plot has exposed places a strain on the fifth act, producing a peculiar shiftiness of tone and mode." See " 'The Sign and Semblance of Her Honor': Reading Gender Difference in *Much Ado about Nothing*," *PMLA* 101, no. 2 (March 1986): 197–98. This is one of the most thoughtful and penetrating essays on *Much Ado about Nothing* in recent years.

18. Northrop Frye, *A Natural Perspective: The Development of Shakespearean Comedy and Romance* (New York: Harcourt, Brace and World, 1965), 128.

19. Alexander Leggatt remarks, "But the most important aspect of [the Watch's] role . . . is their utter detachment from the issues and feelings—even from the facts—of the plot they accidentally unravel. Shakespeare is at pains to see that Don John's mischief is undone not by a change of heart in the erring characters, or by the intelligent intervention of Hero's friends, but by the impersonal workings of the plot, the machinery of accident and coincidence unintentionally set in motion by the clowns"; see *Shakespeare's Comedy of Love,* 162.

20. It is a large part of John A. Allen's essay on Dogberry, cited above, to establish the parallels between the constable and the putatively superior principals of *Much Ado about Nothing.*

21. J. Dennis Huston has expressed the dissatisfaction succinctly: "The characters at the end of *Much Ado about Nothing* show a decided tendency to fix the blame almost entirely in a single source—Don John—as if human suffering were caused exclusively by some locatable evil-doer who can be identified and rooted out of society. Such an attitude conspicuously ignores the other human weaknesses which variously contribute to this suffering"; see *Shakespeare's Comedies of Play* (New York: Columbia University Press, 1981), 123.

*Chapter Six*

1. The phrase is used repeatedly in *Shakespeare's Festive Comedy* and is central to Barber's argument.

2. This distinction is well addressed by Edward Berry: "In Shakespearean comedy the crucial obstacles are usually psychological, not social or metaphysical"; see *Shakespeare's Comic Rites* (Cambridge: Cambridge University Press, 1984), 9.

3. At its most simplistic and cynical the pastoral vision could become an aristocratic attempt to deny the very real sufferings of the underclasses. The English economy of Shakespeare's day really was pastoral in that the raising of wool for export was a central and lucrative industry. The enclosures of arable land to create pasture in the sixteenth century had effected the economies of scale necessary for the

profitable export of wool, but only at the price of driving from the land thousands of laborers suddenly at a loss for the means to live. On the economic and historical conditions in which the production of pastoral poetry was embedded, see Louis Adrian Montrose, "Of Gentlemen and Shepherds: The Politics of Elizabethan Pastoral Form," *ELH* 50, no. 3 (Fall 1983): 415–59.

4. The adjective in quotation marks derives from the title of Lyly's highly popular protonovel *Euphues; or, The Anatomy of Wit* (1579), a work written in an ornate and sententious prose, which, among other things, makes elaborate use of antithesis. The style became a literary fad, and Shakespeare has some wonderfully parodic fun with it in *1 Henry IV*, II.iv.398–419.

5. *As You Like It*, III.ii. I am indebted here and elsewhere to C. L. Barber for pointing out the way Touchstone's exchange with the shepherd Corin in this scene works to foreground the contradictory wishes of the pastoral genre itself; see *Shakespeare's Festive Comedy*, 227.

6. In Lodge's *Rosalynde*, for instance, the labor of the heroines-turned-shepherds is barely more than a formula for temporal punctuation, the end of an episode (and a day) being signaled by some such phrase as "With that they put their Sheepe into the coates." See *Rosalynde* in *Narrative and Dramatic Sources of Shakespeare*, 8 vols., ed. Geoffrey Bullough (London: Routledge and Kegan Paul, 1958), 2: 158–256.

7. I use "frame" here in something like the sense the sociologist uses it in analyzing social situations and the ways people in daily life have of interpreting them. For a thorough and illuminating discussion of such analysis, see Erving Goffman's *Frame Analysis: An Essay on the Organization of Experience* (Cambridge: Harvard University Press, 1974). Goffman draws many of his most telling examples not from daily life, but from plays, including a number from Shakespearean comedy. Keir Elam's *Shakespeare's Universe of Discourse: Language-Games in the Comedies* (Cambridge: Cambridge University Press, 1984) makes effective use of frame analysis, Goffman's in particular, in analyzing a variety of speech situations in Shakespearean comedy.

8. A. O. Lovejoy and George Boas made a distinction between "hard" and "soft" pastorals, and we could easily accommodate Corin to the first, Silvius to the second. The two kinds tend in practice to shade into one another, a fact that in no way detracts from the shock of the juxtaposition that Shakespeare has arranged here; see *Primitivism and Related Ideas in Antiquity* (Baltimore: Johns Hopkins Press, 1935), 10ff.

9. Touchstone's very name suggests his testing function. A touchstone, of course, is a kind of quartz or jasper used to determine the quality of gold or silver ores according to the color of the streak left when such ores are rubbed on it.

10. Shakespeare would pursue the paradox of the misanthrope in a darker context in his late tragedy *Timon of Athens* (1607–8). In the middle of the seventeenth century the French playwright Molière provided a comic analogy to Jaques in his character Alceste, hero of his comedy *The Misanthrope*. Alceste's headlong

denunciation of humanity is always committing him to a hasty and final retreat, and yet, though he is frequently frozen in the posture of leaving, he never quite leaves. He, like Jaques, is a figure not of solitude and isolation, but of thresholds. Jaques's name, incidentally, suggests the Elizabethan word *jakes,* a privy. It seems well suited to express his view of the world in general.

11. For an illuminating discussion of the defense of satire and the allegations against which that defense was conducted, see Alvin B. Kernan, *The Cankered Muse: Satire of the English Renaissance* (New Haven: Yale University Press, 1959).

12. Edward Berry makes the altogether pertinent distinction between those in *As You Like It* who play roles and those who allow their roles to play them; see *Shakespeare's Comic Rites,* 84.

13. The best account of this fallacious identification is perhaps Lionel Trilling's "Reality in America," in *The Liberal Imagination: Essays on Literature and Society* (New York: Viking Press, 1950), 3–21. As Trilling there remarks, "In this view of things, reality, although always reliable, is always rather sober-sided, even grim" (5). The theme is sounded again in another essay in the same volume, "Manners, Morals, and the Novel," 205–22.

14. There is a further joke in the fact that Orlando's poetry is so feebly conventional, so much like the effusions of hundreds of other sonneteers and love poets, that, apart from Rosalind's reiterated proper name, it could be addressed to virtually any lady. When Cervantes's Don Quixote asks Sanson Carrasco to write some verses on the subject of the Don's parting from his beloved Dulcinea, he directs Sanson to work in an acrostic of his lady's name: "'You must get it in, whichever way you do it,' said Don Quixote, 'because if the name is not there, plain and manifest, no woman will believe that the verses have been made for her'"; see *The Adventures of Don Quixote,* trans. J. M. Cohen (Baltimore: Penguin Books, 1950), 496.

15. The classic study of the institution of the fool in the Middle Ages and Renaissance is Enid Welsford's *The Fool: His Social and Literary History* (London: Faber and Faber, 1935). It has often been observed that the character of fools and fooling in Shakespeare's plays changed toward the end of the 1590s. Clowns like Bottom in *A Midsummer Night's Dream* and Dogberry in *Much Ado about Nothing* produce hilarity without intending to, while Touchstone in the present play and Feste in *Twelfth Night* seem fully alert to and in control of the effects they produce. The shift in the role of fool has been interpreted as Shakespeare's way of accommodating the peculiar talents of Robert Armin, who succeeded Will Kempe as chief clown of the Lord Chamberlain's Men. For an account of "dry" and "sly" fools and their different effects on dramatic illusion and audience response, see Maynard Mack, "Engagement and Detachment in Shakespeare's Plays," 288.

16. An observation of Mikhail Bakhtin's seems to catch the fool's unique relation to language: "The creating consciousness stands, as it were, on the boundary line between languages and styles"; see *The Dialogic Imagination. Four Essays,* ed. Michael Holquist, trans. Caryl Emerson and Michael Holquist (Austin: University

of Texas Press, 1981), 60. The remark is cited by Wolfgang Iser in "The Dramatization of Double Meaning in Shakespeare's *As You Like It*," *Theatre Journal* 35,
no. 3 (October 1983): 307–32. Iser describes the fool's discourse as "a form of language that wrecks the pragmatic finality of the dialogue" (329). The present argument is indebted to this difficult but illuminating essay.

*Chapter Seven*

1. For an extended discussion of narcissistic self-love in *Twelfth Night*, see
Joseph Westlund, *Shakespeare's Reparative Comedies: A Psychoanalytic View of the
Middle Plays* (Chicago: University of Chicago Press, 1984), 93–119.

2. Alexander Leggatt remarks, "For Orsino, all activities (including love itself) are swallowed up by the language that expresses them, and the result is a life of
words alone, with no hope of action"; see *Shakespeare's Comedy of Love*, 228.

3. In her introduction to *The Riverside Shakespeare* text of *Twelfth Night*
Anne Barton remarks of the passage in which Valentine describes Olivia's mourning to Orsino, "The underlying image here is homely, even a little grotesque. Like a
housewife who carefully turns a piece of pickled meat once a day in its brine bath,
Olivia intends through salt tears to preserve the memory of her dead brother beyond the normal span of grief"; see *The Riverside Shakespeare*, 405.

4. C. L. Barber cogently remarks, "The effect of moving back and forth
from woman to sprightly page is to convey how much the sexes differ yet how much
they have in common, how everyone who is fully alive has qualities of both"; see
*Shakespeare's Festive Comedy*, 247.

5. Such inversions are incisively treated by Terence Eagleton, in "Language and
Reality in *Twelfth Night*," *Critical Quarterly* 9, no. 3 (Autumn 1967): 217–28.

6. Lewis Carroll said, "Words mean more than we mean to express when we
use them"; cited by James R. Kincaid in his introduction to *Alice's Adventures in
Wonderland* (Berkeley and Los Angeles: University of California Press, 1982), 7.

7. Barber observes, "This supremely feminine damsel, who 'sat like patience on a monument,' is not Viola. She is a sort of polarity within Viola"; see
*Shakespeare's Festive Comedy*, 247. But Barber may overstate the case for the instru-
mentality of Viola's active side. In spite of her role she remains subordinate to time
and chance, and her comparison of herself to an allegorical statue suggests not so
much a "polarity" within her, as a possibility of her still uncertain situation, the possibility that the self, having missed the opportunity for love, will simply dwindle
into a paralyzed attitude.

8. The reader is once again referred to Wolfgang Iser's essay, "The Dramatization of Double Meaning in Shakespeare's *As You Like It*."

9. On attempts to legislate meaning according to individual will, see
Ronald R. Macdonald, "Uneasy Lies: Language and History in Shakespeare's Lan-
castrian Tetralogy," *Shakespeare Quarterly* 35, no. 1 (Spring 1984): 22–39.

10. For a brief account of reaction-formation, see Freud's "Character and
Anal Erotism" (1908), *S.E.* 9: 169–75.

11. The romantic essayist Charles Lamb, in what is now generally considered a wrongheaded view of Malvolio, found his character "cold, austere, repelling" but also "dignified, consistent"; see Lamb's 1822 essay "On Some of the Old Actors" in *Essays of Elia* (London: Arthur L. Humphreys, 1911), 248. We will continue to see that it is precisely Malvolio's inconsistency, the divisions within him, that generate the often brittle comedy in those parts of *Twelfth Night* where he is dominant.

12. The issue of will is, of course, a central one in *Twelfth Night*. The play's subtitle (the only one in the canon) is *What You Will*, which seems to extend an invitation similar to *As You Like It:* "make of this what you please." But the play is also concerned with darker matters such as the will to power, the corrupt will in league with the imagination, the delusion of mastery. Malvolio's very name means "bad will."

13. Stephen Booth argues that the forged letter presents Malvolio with overwhelming evidence that it has, indeed, come from Olivia and that we should be slow to call his interpretation delusional, at least in a play where we have accepted without demur the fact that she has fallen in love with a young woman disguised as a young man, and one she takes for a servant at that. And yet Malvolio does need to "crush" the string of initials a little to make it "bow" to him (II.v.140). See "*Twelfth Night:* 1.1: The Audience as Malvolio," in *Shakespeare's "Rough Magic,"* 149–67.

14. For a brilliant discussion of uncrowning and carnival, see Mikhail Bakhtin, *Rabelais and His World,* trans. Helene Iswolsky (Cambridge: M.I.T. Press, 1968).

15. For an illuminating discussion of Feste's remarkable whirligig and its ironic relation to Malvolio's fate, see Joan Hartwig, "Feste's 'Whirligig' and the Comic Providence of *Twelfth Night,*" *ELH* 40, no. 4 (Winter 1973): 501–13.

16. This soliloquy is central to Barber's argument not just in his chapter on *Henry IV,* but in the argument of *Shakespeare's Festive Comedy* as a whole. It is the relation between holiday and everyday, not the one or the other considered in isolation, that is meaningful. For an anthropological argument neatly parallel to Barber's, see Victor W. Turner, *The Ritual Process: Structure and Anti-Structure* (Chicago: Aldine Publishing, 1973).

17. Ralph Berry, "*Twelfth Night:* The Experience of the Audience," *Shakespeare Survey* 34 (1981): 119.

18. Terence Eagleton remarks of the dark room episode, "Illusion . . . both defines a man falsely and negates as false any criterion beyond itself to which appeal can be made: it is a kind of language which, by collapsing and controlling reality within itself, can adjust it endlessly for its own purposes. Illusion and language create a structure whose roles operate to control, not only the experience within the structure, but any possible experience outside it"; see "Language and Reality in *Twelfth Night,*" 224.

19. Leo Salingar has put the matter well: "*Twelfth Night* is the summing-up of a major phase in Shakespeare's comic writing, the last romantic play at the end of a decade, because it deals with the psychological value of revelry and its limits as

well; it is a comedy about comedy. It illustrates at once his fundamental debt to the earlier Renaissance tradition of comic playwriting and his abiding sense of detachment from 'it"; see *Shakespeare and the Traditions of Comedy* (Cambridge: Cambridge University Press, 1974), 242.

20. Joan Hartwig makes a similar point in "Feste's 'Whirligig' and the Comic Providence of *Twelfth Night.*"

*Conclusion*

1. The editors of the First Folio of 1623 classified the final plays variously. The table of contents lists *The Winter's Tale* and *The Tempest* under comedies, *Cymbeline* under tragedies, and omits mention of *Pericles* altogether. The text of the last-named play is omitted as well.

2. Frye, *Anatomy of Criticism,* 163.

3. See "The Study of Poetry" (1880), in *The Complete Prose Works of Matthew Arnold,* 11 vols., ed. R. H. Super (Ann Arbor: University of Michigan Press, 1960–77), 9:177.

# Selected Bibliography

## PRIMARY WORKS

About half of Shakespeare's plays appeared individually in quartos, some with good texts, some clearly piracies or memorial reconstructions. Modern editions rely on quartos, where good ones exist, and the First Folio of 1623, compiled seven years after Shakespeare's death by two former members of his company, John Heminge and Henry Condell. This contains the whole canon, with the exception of *Pericles*. The following are the first reliable printed versions of the comedies, exclusive of the problem plays. Titles from the First Folio are head-titles.

*As You Like It.* First Folio, 1623.
*The Comedie of Errors.* First Folio, 1623.
*A Pleasant Conceited Comedie Called Loues labors lost. As it was presented before her Highnes this last Christmas. Newly corrected and augmented by W. Shakespeare.* First Quarto, 1598.
*The most excellent Historie of the Merchant of Venice. With the extreame crueltie of Shylocke the Iewe towards the sayd Merchant, in cutting a iust pound of his flesh: and the obtayning of Portia by the choyse of three chests. As it hath beene divers times acted by the Lord Chamberlaine his Seruants.* First Quarto, 1600.
*The Merry Wiues of Windsor.* First Folio, 1623.
*A Midsommer nights dreame. As it hath beene sundry times publickely acted, by the Right honourable, the Lord Chamberlaine his seruants.* First Quarto, 1600.
*Much adoe about Nothing. As it hath been sundrie times publikely acted by the right honourable, the Lord Chamberlaine his seruants. Written by William Shakespeare.* First Quarto, 1600.
*The Taming of the Shrew.* First Folio, 1623.
*Twelfe Night, Or what you will.* First Folio, 1623.
*The Two Gentlemen of Verona.* First Folio, 1623.

## SECONDARY WORKS

The following are selected indeed, for the literature on Shakespeare's comedies is dauntingly large and keeps growing, although one even now abetting this process has no real right to complain. The bibliography number of *Shakespeare Quarterly* covering 1989, for instance, contains just under 5,000 entries.

Barber, C. L. *Shakespeare's Festive Comedy: A Study of Dramatic Form and Its Relation to Social Custom.* 1959. Reprint. Princeton: Princeton University Press, 1972. This is one of the most influential books on Shakespearean comedy of this century. It argues a dialectical relation between everyday and holiday, seriousness and foolery. No student of Shakespeare's comedies should overlook it.

Berry, Edward I. *Shakespeare's Comic Rites.* Cambridge: Cambridge University Press, 1984. A level-headed, sensible, and illuminating approach that looks at the plays from the point of view of rites of passage.

Burckhardt, Sigurd. *Shakespearean Meanings.* Princeton: Princeton University Press, 1968. A posthumous collection of Burckhardt's writings on Shakespeare, only one of which, an essay on *The Merchant of Venice,* is directly related to comedy. But Burckhardt was so inventive, unsentimental, and illuminating that his work is pertinent to anyone interested in any aspect of the plays, comedy very much included.

Calderwood, James L. *Shakespearean Metadrama: The Argument of the Play in "Titus Adronicus," "Love's Labour's Lost," "Romeo and Juliet," "A Midsummer Night's Dream," and "Richard II."* Minneapolis: University of Minnesota Press, 1971. A pioneering study in what has since become a familiar topic: the ways in which Shakespeare's plays can be said to be about themselves. Calderwood is temperate and provides excellent readings of the two comedies he treats.

Carroll, William C. *The Metamorphoses of Shakespearean Comedy.* Princeton: Princeton University Press, 1985. A generous study of selected comedies with a concluding chapter on metamorphosis in the late romances, providing some interesting links between these closely related genres. Carroll has also written a very valuable book-length study of *Love's Labor's Lost, The Great Feast of Language in "Love's Labour's Lost,"* (Princeton: Princeton University Press, 1976).

Danson, Lawrence. *The Harmonies of "The Merchant of Venice."* New Haven: Yale University Press, 1978. Presents a view of this play from which the present study very much dissents, but the book is nicely argued and historically informed.

Duckworth, George. *The Nature of Roman Comedy.* Princeton: Princeton University Press, 1952. A magisterial and classic account of the history and development of Latin comedy.

Eagleton, Terry. *William Shakespeare.* London: Basil Blackwell, 1986. Provocative, often outrageous, Marxist-deconstructionist readings of six Shakespearean comedies, with more of the same for selected histories and tragedies.

Elam, Keir. *Shakespeare's Universe of Discourse: Language-Games in the Comedies.* Cambridge: Cambridge University Press, 1984. A somewhat technical, but very interesting, study of language patterns and what they do. Highly focused examples move the reader constantly across the whole span of Shakespearean comedy.

Erickson, Peter, and Coppélia Kahn, eds. *Shakespeare's "Rough Magic": Renaissance Essays in Honor of C. L. Barber.* Newark: University of Delaware Press, 1985. Contains a number of cogent essays on the comedies, including Janet Adelman's essay on male bonding in the comedies in general and Stephen Booth's provocative essay on *Twelfth Night.*

Evans, Bertrand. *Shakespeare's Comedies.* Oxford: Clarendon Press, 1960. A sensible survey concentrating on disparities in awareness between audience and characters.

Evans, Malcolm. *Signifying Nothing: Truth's True Contents in Shakespeare's Text.* Athens: University of Georgia Press, 1986. An irreverent and wry commentary, somewhat in Terry Eagleton's manner (see above), that suggests, among other things, that all of Shakespeare's comedies, not just the ones usually so designated, are really "problem plays."

Frye, Northrop. *Anatomy of Criticism: Four Essays.* Princeton: Princeton University Press, 1957. A modern classic. In a long and prolific career Frye had perhaps more to say about the comic genre than about any other. The essay included here, "The Mythos of Spring: Comedy," is most pertinent. Its views are neatly summed up in a short essay, "The Argument of Comedy," in *English Institute Essays 1948,* ed. D. A. Robertson, Jr. (New York: Columbia University Press, 1949), 58–73. Frye also devoted a short book exclusively to Shakespearean comedy and romance, *A Natural Perspective: The Development of Shakespearean Comedy and Romance* (New York: Harcourt, Brace and World, 1965).

Garber, Marjorie. *Coming of Age in Shakespeare.* London: Methuen, 1981. Like Edward Berry's book (see above), a look at comic development in terms of rites of passage. But Garber's argument is much more informed by psychoanalysis and is particularly good on the relation of naming to individuation.

Huston, J. Dennis. *Shakespeare's Comedies of Play.* New York: Columbia University Press, 1981. Lively and thoughtful readings of *The Comedy of Errors, Love's Labor's Lost, The Taming of the Shrew, A Midsummer Night's Dream,* and *Much Ado about Nothing.*

Iser, Wolfgang. "The Dramatization of Double Meaning in Shakespeare's *As You Like It.*" *Theater Journal* 35, no. 3 (October 1983): 307–32. This essay, much indebted to the work of Mikhail Bakhtin, is difficult but very rewarding. Although it focuses exclusively on *As You Like It,* the discussion of utterance without pragmatic intent is pertinent to all the comedies and to a good bit of Shakespearean drama in general.

Johnson, Samuel. *Johnson on Shakespeare.* 2 vols. Edited by Arthur Sherbo. New Haven: Yale University Press, 1968. This is the Shakespearean work of the great eighteenth-century essayist and lexicographer. The "Preface" to Johnson's edition of the complete works is a monument of the critical tradition. Johnson was the first to reject in a cogent way the strictures of neo-Aristotelian formalism in approaching Shakespearean drama. These volumes, separately subtitled, are actually the seventh and eighth in *The Yale Edition of the Works of Samuel Johnson*, 15 vols., ed. E. L. McAdam, Jr., with Donald Hyde and Mary Hyde (New Haven: Yale University Press, 1958–78).

Kermode, Frank. "The Mature Comedies." In *Early Shakespeare, Stratford-upon-Avon Studies*, vol. 3, edited by John Russell Brown and Bernard Harris, 211–27. New York: St. Martin's Press, 1961. A fine discussion of the value and complexity of Shakespeare's early comic work.

Leggatt, Alexander. *Shakespeare's Comedy of Love*. London: Methuen, 1974. An intelligent survey of all Shakespeare's comedies, *The Comedy of Errors* through *Twelfth Night*, which is particularly sensitive to the increasingly dark implications that insinuate themselves.

Levin, Richard A. *Love and Society in Shakespearean Comedy*. Newark: University of Delaware Press, 1985. A revisionist look at the comedies with an eye to exclusion and scapegoating. Sometimes overstated, but basically sound.

MacCary, W. Thomas. *Friends and Lovers: The Phenomenology of Desire in Shakespearean Comedy*. A study of the problem of identity in comedy approached from a psychoanalytic perspective, and a very illuminating one.

McFarland, Thomas. *Shakespeare's Pastoral Comedy*. Chapel Hill: University of North Carolina Press, 1972. A solid study of a very important topic, the intertwining of pastoral elements in the comedies.

Righter, Anne. *Shakespeare and the Idea of the Play*. 1962. Reprint. Westport, Conn.: Greenwood Press, 1977. An early attempt at metadramatic criticism, though the author does not use the term. This is an informed scholarly and historical exploration of Shakespeare's reflection on his medium, his language, and his own talent.

Salingar, Leo. *Shakespeare and the Traditions of Comedy*. Cambridge: Cambridge University Press, 1974. Undoubtedly the best exploration of the historical background of Shakespeare's comic work. The scholarship is unexceptionable, the insights many and fine.

Segal, Erich. *Roman Laughter: The Comedy of Plautus*. Cambridge: Harvard University Press, 1968. This is a fine overview and analysis of the elder statesman of Roman comedy.

Van Laan, Thomas F. *Role-Playing in Shakespeare*. Toronto: University of Toronto Press, 1978. This is by now a familiar topic, but it is here handled with intelligence and an insight that produces some important distinctions.

Weimann, Robert. *Shakespeare and the Popular Tradition in the Theater: Studies in the Social Dimension of Dramatic Form and Function*. Rev. ed. Baltimore: Johns Hopkins University Press, 1978. This somewhat overlooked study of the complex traditions of representation Shakespeare inherited is a central document for understanding the institution of foolery and how it differs from the mimetic style to which we are accustomed.

**Westlund, Joseph.** *Shakespeare's Reparative Comedies: A Psychoanalytic View of the Middle Plays.* Chicago: University of Chicago Press, 1984. A modest but very interesting study, particularly of narcissism as a stage in development.

**Young, David P.** *Something of Great Constancy: The Art of "A Midsummer Night's Dream."* New Haven: Yale University Press, 1966. This is a graceful study of the play and one that is particularly sensitive to complex patternings. Its introductory chapter on the Tudor background of this comedy is excellent. Young has also written a study of Shakespeare's pastoralism, *The Heart's Forest: A Study of Shakespeare's Pastoral Plays* (New Haven: Yale University Press, 1972). This is valuable in part because it deals with *King Lear, The Winter's Tale,* and *The Tempest,* as well as with *As You Like It.* It thus provides some links among comedies, tragedies, and romances.

# Index

# The Author

Ronald R. Macdonald received his B.A. from Yale College (1966) and his Ph.D. from the Yale University Graduate School (1983). He taught for a year at Yale in 1966–67 as a Carnegie Teaching Fellow in English, and since 1971 he has taught English Renaissance literature, American literature, and genre studies at Smith College, where he is an associate professor of English. In addition to articles on Shakespeare and others, he is the author of *The Burial-Places of Memory: Epic Underworlds in Vergil, Dante, and Milton* (Amherst: University of Massachusetts Press, 1987). Professor Macdonald is a member of the editorial board of *English Literary Renaissance* and a member of the International Committee for the World Shakespeare Bibliography.

ISBN 0-8057-7010-0

90000

9 780805 770100